HEAVEN I

DR. JAEROCK LEE

CREATION
HOUSE
A STRANG COMPANY

HEAVEN I by Dr. Jaerock Lee
Published by Creation House
A Strang Company
600 Rinehart Road
Lake Mary, Florida 32746
www.creationhouse.com

Unless otherwise noted, all Scripture quotations are from the Holy Bible, New International Version. Copyright © 1973, 1978, 1984, International Bible Society. Used by permission.

Publisher's Note: The views expressed in this book are not necessarily the views held by the publisher.

Cover design by Terry Clifton

Previously published by Urim Books, Seoul, Korea. Copyright © 2002, ISBN: 89-7557-046-0, ISBN: 89-7557-045-2(set). Translated by Dr. Kooyoung Chung. Used by permission.

Library of Congress Control Number: 2006926083
International Standard Book Number: 1-59979-018-1

First Edition

06 07 08 09 10 — 987654321
Printed in the United States of America

CONTENTS

FOREWORD

Hoping that each of you will realize God's patient love, accomplish the whole spirit, and run toward New Jerusalem.

I give all the thanks and glory to God who has led numerous people to know about the spiritual realm properly and run toward the goal with a hope for heaven through the publication of *Hell* and the two-part series *Heaven*.

This book consists of ten chapters and lets you know clearly about the life, beauty, different places of heaven, and rewards given according to the measure of faith. This is what God has revealed to the Reverend Dr. Jaerock Lee by the inspiration of the Holy Spirit.

Chapter 1, "Heaven: As Clear and Beautiful As Crystal," describes the eternal happiness of heaven by looking at general appearances of it, where there will be no need for any sun or moon to shine.

Chapter 2, "The Garden of Eden and the Waiting Place of Heaven," explains the location, appearances, and life in the Garden of Eden, to help you better understand heaven. This chapter also tells you about the plan and providence of God in His having put the tree of the knowledge of good and evil and cultivating human beings spiritually. Moreover, it tells you about the Waiting Place where saved people wait until the Judgment Day. It details life in that place, and what kind of people enter New Jerusalem straightaway without waiting there.

Chapter 3, "The Seven-Year Wedding Banquet," explains Jesus Christ's Second Advent, the Seven-Year

Great Tribulation, the Lord's coming back to the earth, the Millennium, and eternal life after that.

Chapter 4, "Secrets of Heaven Hidden Since the Creation," covers the secrets of heaven that came to be unveiled by the parables of Jesus. It teaches you how to possess heaven, where there are many dwelling places.

Chapter 5, "How Will We Live in Heaven?" explains the height, weight, and skin color of the spiritual body, and how we will live. With various examples of joyous life in heaven, this chapter also urges you to forcefully advance toward heaven with a great hope for it.

Chapter 6, "Paradise," explains Paradise that is the lowest level of heaven, yet happier and much more beautiful than this world. It also describes the kind of people who will enter Paradise.

Chapter 7, "The First Kingdom of Heaven," explains the life and rewards of the First Kingdom, which will house those who accepted Jesus Christ and tried to live according to God's Word.

Chapter 8, "The Second Kingdom of Heaven," delves into the life and rewards of the Second Kingdom where those who did not accomplish holiness completely but did their duties will enter. It also emphasizes the importance of obedience and performing one's duty.

Chapter 9, "The Third Kingdom of Heaven," explains the beauty and glory of the Third Kingdom, which cannot be compared to the Second Kingdom. The Third Kingdom is the place for only those who threw away all their sins—even sins in their nature—by their own efforts and the help of the Holy Spirit. It explains the love of God who allows tests and trials.

Lastly, Chapter 10, "New Jerusalem," introduces New Jerusalem, the most beautiful and glorious place in heaven, where God's throne is located. It describes the kind of people who will enter New Jerusalem. This chapter closes by providing readers with a hope through the examples of the houses of two people who will enter New Jerusalem.

God has prepared heaven, which is as clear and beautiful as crystal for His beloved children. He wants many people to be saved and looks forward to seeing His children enter New Jerusalem.

I hope, in the name of the Lord, that all readers of *Heaven I: As Clear and Beautiful as Crystal* will realize God's great love, accomplish the whole spirit with the Lord's heart, and run toward New Jerusalem vigorously.

—GEUMSUN VIN
DIRECTOR OF EDITORIAL BUREAU, URIM BOOKS

PREFACE

THE GOD OF love not only leads every believer to the way of salvation but also reveals the secrets of heaven.

At least once in a lifetime, one probably has questions like: "Where am I going after life in this world?" or "Do heaven and hell really exist?"

Many people die even before they find answers to such questions. Even if they believe in the afterlife, not everyone possesses heaven, because not everyone has the proper knowledge. Heaven and hell are not a fantasy, but a reality in the spiritual realm.

On the one hand, heaven is such a beautiful place that cannot be compared with anything in this world. The beauty and the happiness in New Jerusalem, where God's throne is located, cannot be adequately described because it is made of the best materials and with heavenly skills.

On the other hand, hell is full of endless, tragic pain and everlasting punishment; its horrible reality is explained in detail in my book entitled *Hell*. Heaven and hell came to be known through Jesus and the apostles, and even today they are revealed in detail through the people of God who have sincere faith in Him.

Heaven is the place where the children of God enjoy eternal life, and unimaginable, beautiful, and wondrous things are prepared for them. So you know it in detail only when God permits and shows it to you.

I prayed and fasted continually for seven years to know about heaven and began to receive answers from God. Now God is showing me more of the secrets in the spiritual realm in greater depth.

1

HEAVEN I

Because heaven is not visible, it is very difficult to describe heaven with the language and knowledge of this world. There could also be misunderstandings about it. That is why apostle Paul could not tell in detail about the Paradise in the Third Heaven that he had seen in a vision.

God also taught me a lot of secrets about heaven, and for many months I preached about the happy life and various places and rewards in heaven according to the measure of faith. However, I could not preach all that I have learned in detail.

The reason God lets me make the secrets of the spiritual realm known through this book is to save as many souls as possible and lead them to heaven, which is clear and beautiful as crystal.

I give all the thanks and glory to God for allowing me to publish *Heaven I: As Clear and Beautiful as Crystal*, a description of a place that is filled with God's glory. I hope you will realize God's great desire to show you the secrets of heaven, and that it will lead all people to the way of salvation. I hope you can possess it, too. I also hope you will run toward the goal of an eternal life in New Jerusalem.

I give thanks to Geumsun Vin, director of the editorial bureau, her staff, and the translation bureau for their hard work in the publication of this book. I pray in the name of the Lord that through this book many souls will be saved and enjoy the eternal life in New Jerusalem.

—Dr. Jaerock Lee

CHAPTER 1
HEAVEN: AS CLEAR AND BEAUTIFUL AS CRYSTAL

Then the angel showed me the river of the water of life, as clear as crystal, flowing from the throne of God and of the Lamb down the middle of the great street of the city. On each side of the river stood the tree of life, bearing twelve crops of fruit, yielding its fruit every month. And the leaves of the tree are for the healing of the nations. No longer will there be any curse. The throne of God and of the Lamb will be in the city, and his servants will serve him. They will see his face, and his name will be on their foreheads. There will be no more night. They will not need the light of a lamp or the light of the sun, for the Lord God will give them light. And they will reign for ever and ever.

—REVELATION 22:1–5

Many people wonder and ask, "It is said we can have a happy life eternally in heaven—what kind of place is it?" If you listen to the testimonies of those who have been to heaven, you can hear that most of them have passed through a long tunnel. This is because heaven is in the spiritual realm, which is very different from the world in which you live.

Those who are living in this three-dimensional world do not know about heaven in detail. You know about this wondrous world, above the three-dimensional world, only when God tells you about it or when your spiritual eyes are opened. If you know about this spiritual realm in detail, not only will your soul be happy, but also your faith will quickly grow and

3

you will be beloved by God. Thus, Jesus told you the secrets of heaven through many parables and the apostle John explains about heaven in detail in the Book of Revelation.

Then, what kind of place is heaven and how are people going to live there? You will briefly have a look at heaven, as clear and beautiful as crystal, which God has prepared to share His love with His children eternally.

NEW HEAVEN AND NEW EARTH

The first heaven and the first earth that God had created were as clear and beautiful as crystal, but they were cursed due to the disobedience of Adam, the first man. Also, rapid and expansive industrialization and development in science and technology have polluted this earth, and nowadays more people are calling for the protection of nature.

Therefore, when the time comes, God will set aside the first heaven and the first earth and reveal a new heaven and a new earth. Even though this earth has become polluted and rotten, it is still necessary for raising true children of God who can and will enter heaven.

In the beginning, God created the earth and then a man. He led the man to the Garden of Eden. He gave him maximum freedom and abundance, allowing him everything but eating from the tree of the knowledge of good and evil. The man, however, violated the only thing God had forbidden and was subsequently driven out to this earth, the first heaven and the first earth.

Because the almighty God had known that the human race would go the way of death, He had prepared Jesus Christ even before time began and sent Him down to this earth at the appropriate time.

Thus, whoever accepts Jesus Christ who was crucified and resurrected will be transformed into a new creation and go to the new heaven and the new earth and enjoy an eternal life.

Blue sky of the new heaven as clear as crystal

The sky of the new heaven that God has prepared is filled with clean air to make it truly clear, pure, and unlike the air in this world. Imagine a clear and high sky with pure white clouds. How wonderful and lovely it would be!

Then why will God make the new sky blue? Spiritually, the color blue makes you feel depth, height, and purity. Water that is pure looks blue. As you look at the blue sky, you can also feel your heart refreshed. God made the sky of this world look blue because He made your heart clean and gave you the heart to look for the Creator. If you can confess, looking at the blue, clear sky, "My Creator must be up there. He made everything so beautiful!" your heart will be cleansed and you will be compelled to lead a good life.

What if the whole sky were yellow? Instead of feeling comfortable, people would feel uneasy and confused, and some might even suffer from mental problems. Likewise, people's minds can be moved, refreshed, or confused according to different colors. That is why God has made the sky of the new heaven blue and placed in it pure white clouds so that His children would be able to live happily with hearts that are as clear and beautiful as crystal.

New earth of heaven made of pure gold and jewels

Then, what will the new earth in heaven be like? On the new earth of heaven, which God has made clean and clear as crystal, there is no soil or dust. The new earth is composed only of pure gold and jewels. How fascinating it would be to be in heaven where there are shiny roads made of pure gold and jewels!

Our earth is made of soil, which can be changed over time. This change lets you know about meaninglessness and death. God allowed all the plants to grow, bear fruit, and perish in the soil so that you may realize that life has an end on this earth.

Heaven I

Heaven is made of pure gold and jewels that do not change because heaven is a true and eternal world. Also, just as plants grow on this earth, they will grow in heaven when planted. However, they never die or perish unlike the ones of this earth.

Moreover, even hills and castles are made of pure gold and jewels. How shiny and beautiful they would be! You should have a true faith so that you will not miss out on this beauty and happiness of heaven that cannot be adequately expressed with any words.

Disappearance of the first heaven and the first earth

What will happen to the first heaven and first earth when this beautiful new heaven and new earth appear?

> Then I saw a great white throne and him who was seated on it. Earth and sky fled from his presence, and there was no place for them.
>
> —REVELATION 20:11

> Then I saw a new heaven and a new earth, for the first heaven and the first earth had passed away, and there was no longer any sea.
>
> —REVELATION 21:1

When the people cultivated on this earth are judged between good and evil, the first heaven and the first earth will pass away. This means that they will not disappear completely but instead be relocated to another place.

Then, why will God move the first heaven and the first earth instead of getting rid of them completely? That is because His children living in heaven will miss the first heaven and the first earth if He completely removes them. Even though they had suffered sorrow and hardships in the first heaven and the first earth, they will sometimes miss them because they had once been their home. Thus, knowing this, the God of love moves them to another part in the universe and will not get rid of them completely.

The universe in which you live is an endless world, and there are so many other universes. So God will move the first heaven and the first earth to one corner of the universes and let His children visit them as needed.

There are no tears, sorrow, death, or diseases

The new heaven and the new earth, where children of God saved by faith will live, have no curse again and are full of happiness. In Revelation 21:3–4, you find that there are no tears, sorrow, death, mourning, or diseases in heaven because God is there.

> And I heard a loud voice from the throne saying, "Now the dwelling of God is with men, and he will live with them. They will be his people, and God himself will be with them and be their God. He will wipe every tear from their eyes. There will be no more death or mourning or crying or pain, for the old order of things has passed away."

How sad would it be if you were starving and even your children were crying for food because they were hungry? What would be the use if someone came and said, "You are so hungry that you are shedding your tears," and wiped your tears, but did not give you anything? What, then, would be the real help here? He should give you something to eat so that you and your children will not starve. Only after that will your and your children's tears stop.

Likewise, to say that God will wipe every tear from your eyes means that if you are saved and go to heaven, there will be no more worries or concerns because there are no tears, sorrow, death, mourning, or diseases in heaven.

On the one hand, whether you believe in God or not, you will have to live with some kind of sorrow on this earth. Worldly people will grieve so much even with a little bit of loss they suffer. On the other hand, those who believe will mourn with love and mercy for those who are yet to be saved.

Once you go to heaven, however, you will not have to worry about death or other people's sinning and falling into eternal death. You will not have to suffer from sins, so there cannot be any kind of sorrow.

On this earth when you are filled with sadness you moan. In heaven, however, there is no need for moaning because there will not be any diseases or concerns. There will only be eternal happiness.

THE RIVER OF THE WATER OF LIFE

In heaven, the River of the Water of Life, as clear as crystal, flows in the middle of the great street. Revelation 22:1–2 explains this River of the Water of Life, and you must be happy to just imagine it.

> Then the angel showed me the river of the water of life, as clear as crystal, flowing from the throne of God and of the Lamb down the middle of the great street of the city. On each side of the river stood the tree of life, bearing twelve crops of fruit, yielding its fruit every month. And the leaves of the tree are for the healing of the nations.

I once swam in a very clear sea of the Pacific, and the water was so clear that I could see the plants and fish in it. It was so beautiful that I was so happy to be in it. Even in this world, you can feel your heart getting refreshed and cleansed when you look at clear water. How much happier you would be in heaven where the River of the Water of Life, which is as clear as crystal, flows in the middle of the great street!

The River of the Water of Life

Even in this world, if you look at the clean sea, the sunshine is reflected by the ripples and shines beautifully. The

River of the Water of Life in heaven looks blue from afar, but if you look at it from a closer distance, it is so clear, beautiful, spotless, and pure that you can express it "as clear as crystal."

Why, then, does this River of the Water of Life flow out from the throne of God and of the Lamb? Spiritually, water refers to God's Word, which is the food of life, and you gain eternal life through God's Word. Jesus says in John 4:14, "Whoever drinks the water I give him will never thirst. Indeed, the water I give him will become in him a spring of water welling up to eternal life." God's Word is the water of eternal life that gives life to you, and that is why the River of the Water of Life flows out from the throne of God and of the Lamb.

How, then, will the water of life taste? It is something so sweet that you cannot experience it in this world, and you will feel energized once you drink it. God gave the water of life to human beings, but after the Fall of Adam, water on this earth was cursed along with all other things. Since then, people have not been able to taste the water of life on this earth. You will be able to taste it only after you go to heaven. People on this earth are drinking polluted water, and they look for artificial drinks such as soft drinks instead of water. Likewise, water on this earth can never give eternal life, but the water of life in heaven, God's Word, gives eternal life. It is sweeter than honey and drippings from the honeycomb, and it gives strength to your spirit.

The river flows all around heaven

The River of the Water of Life that flows from the throne of God and the Lamb is just like the blood that sustains life by circulating in your body. It runs all around heaven flowing in the middle of the great street, and comes back to the throne of God. Why, then, does this River of the Water of Life run all around heaven flowing in the middle of the great street?

First of all, this River of the Water of Life is the easiest way to go to God's throne. Therefore, to go to New Jerusalem where God's throne is located, you just follow the street made of pure gold on each side of the river.

Second, within God's Word is the way to heaven and you can enter heaven only when you follow this way of the Word of God. As Jesus says in John 14:6, "I am the way and the truth and the life. No one comes to the Father except through me," there is the way to heaven in God's Word of truth. When you act according to God's Word, you can enter heaven where God's Word, the River of the Water of Life, flows.

Likewise, God designed heaven in such a way that just by following the River of the Water of Life, you can arrive at New Jerusalem, which houses God's throne.

Gold and silver sands on the riverside

What will there be on the side of the River of the Water of Life? You first notice gold and silver sands spread far and wide. Sand in heaven is round and so soft that it will not stick to the clothing at all even if you walk in it.

Also, there are many comfortable benches decorated with gold and jewels. When you sit on the bench with your dear friends and have blissful conversations, pretty angels will serve you.

On this earth, you admire angels, but in heaven angels will call you "master" and serve you as you wish. If you want to have some fruit, the angel will bring fruit in a basket decorated with jewels or flowers and hand the basket over to you in an instant.

Furthermore, on both sides of the River of the Water of Life are beautiful flowers of many colors, birds, insects, and animals. They also serve you as their master, and you can share your love with them. How wonderful and beautiful this heaven is with this River of the Water of Life!

The Tree of Life on each side of the river

Revelation 22:2 explains in detail the tree of life on each side of the River of the Water of Life:

Down the middle of the great street of the city. On each
side of the river stood the tree of life, bearing twelve crops
of fruit, yielding its fruit every month. And the leaves of
the tree are for the healing of the nations.

Why, then, has God placed the tree of life bearing twelve
crops of fruit on each side of the river? Primarily, God wanted
all His children who have entered heaven to feel the beauty
and life of heaven. He also wanted to remind them that they
were bearing the fruit of the Holy Spirit when they acted
according to God's Word, just as they could eat food by the
sweat of their brow.

You have to realize one thing here. Bearing twelve crops
does not mean that one tree bears twelve crops, but twelve
different kinds of trees of life bear each crop. In the Bible, you
can see that twelve tribes of Israel were formed through the
twelve sons of Jacob. Through these twelve tribes the nation
of Israel was formed and the nations that accept Christianity have been erected all over the world. Even Jesus selected
twelve disciples, and the gospel has been preached and spread
to all nations through them and their disciples.

Therefore, twelve crops of the tree of life symbolize that
anyone from any nation, if he follows the faith, can bear the
fruit of the Holy Spirit and enter heaven.

If you eat the beautiful and colorful fruit of the tree of life,
you will be refreshed and feel happier. Also, as soon as it is
picked, another one will replace it, so the fruit never runs out.
The leaves of the tree of life are dark green and shiny, and will
stay that way forever because they are not something to be
fallen or eaten. These green and shiny leaves are much bigger
than leaves of the trees of this world, and they grow in a very
orderly manner.

Heaven I

The Throne of God and of the Lamb

Revelation 22:3–5 describes the location of the throne of God and the Lamb as in the middle of heaven:

> No longer will there be any curse. The throne of God and of the Lamb will be in the city, and his servants will serve him. They will see his face, and his name will be on their foreheads. There will be no more night. They will not need the light of a lamp or the light of the sun, for the Lord God will give them light. And they will reign for ever and ever.

The throne is in the middle of heaven

Heaven is the eternal place where God reigns with love and righteousness. In New Jerusalem, located in the middle of heaven, there is the throne of God and of the Lamb. The Lamb here refers to Jesus Christ (John 1:29; 1 Peter 1:19).

Not everybody can enter the place where God usually stays. It is located in a space of another dimension from New Jerusalem. God's throne in this place is so much more beautiful and brighter than the one in New Jerusalem.

God's throne in New Jerusalem is where God Himself comes down when His children worship or have banquets. Revelation 4:2–3 explains God's sitting on His throne:

> At once I was in the Spirit, and there before me was a throne in heaven with someone sitting on it. And the one who sat there had the appearance of jasper and carnelian. A rainbow, resembling an emerald, encircled the throne.

Around the throne are twenty-four elders sitting, clothed in white garments with golden crowns on their heads. Before the throne are the seven spirits of God and the sea of glass, clear as crystal. In the center and around the throne are the four living creatures and many heavenly hosts and angels.

Furthermore, God's throne is covered with lights. It is so beautiful, amazing, majestic, dignified, and huge that it is beyond human comprehension. Also, on the right side of God's throne is the throne of the Lamb, our Lord Jesus. It is definitely different from the throne of God, but God the Trinity, the Father, the Son, and the Holy Spirit, has the same heart, characteristics, and power.

More details about God's throne will be explained in my second book about heaven entitled *Filled With God's Glory*.

No night and no day

God reigns over heaven and the universe with His love and justice from His throne, which is bright with the holy and beautiful light of glory. The throne is in the middle of heaven. Beside the throne of God is the throne of the Lamb, and it also shines the light of glory. Therefore, heaven does not need the sun or the moon, or any other light or electricity to shine on it. There is no night or day in heaven.

By the way, Hebrews 12:14 urges you to "make every effort to live in peace with all men and to be holy; without holiness no one will see the Lord." Jesus in Matthew 5:8 promises you that "blessed are the pure in heart, for they will see God."

Therefore, those believers who get rid of all the evil from their hearts and completely obey God's Word will see the face of God. To the extent that they resemble the Lord, believers will be blessed in this world and live closer to God's throne in heaven as well.

How happy people will be if they can see God's face, serve Him, and share love with Him forever! However, just as you cannot look at the sun directly because of its brightness, those who do not resemble the heart of the Lord cannot see God from a close distance.

Enjoying true happiness forever in heaven

You can enjoy true happiness in anything you do in heaven because it is the best gift God has prepared with an exceeding love for His children. Angels will serve the children of God, as it says in Hebrews 1:14: "Are not all angels ministering spirits sent to serve those who will inherit salvation?" As people have different measures of faith, however, the size of the houses and the number of ministering angels will differ according to the extent that the people resemble God.

They will be served like princes or princesses because the angels will read the minds of their masters to whom they are assigned and prepare anything they want. Moreover, animals and plants will love the children of God and serve them. Animals in heaven possess no evil. They will obey God's children unconditionally and sometimes try to do cute things to please them.

How about the plants in heaven? Each plant has a beautiful and unique scent and whenever God's children approach them, they give out that scent. Flowers give off the best scent for God's children, and the scent even spreads to distant places. The scent is also regenerated as soon as it is given out.

Also, the fruits of the twelve kinds of tree of life have tastes of their own. If you smell the scent of the flowers or eat from the tree of life, you will become so refreshed and happy that it cannot be compared with anything in this world.

Furthermore, unlike the plants of this earth, flowers in heaven will smile when children of God approach them. They will even dance for their masters, and the people can have conversations with them as well.

Even if somebody picks a flower, it will not be hurt or sad but be restored by the power of God. The flower that is picked will be dissolved into the air and disappear. The fruit eaten by people will also be dissolved as beautiful scents and disappear through breathing.

There are four seasons in heaven, and people can enjoy the change of seasons. People will feel the love of God enjoying the special features of each season: spring, summer, fall, and winter. Now one may ask, "Would we still suffer from the hotness of summer and the coldness of winter even in heaven?" The weather in heaven, however, forms the most perfect condition for God's children to live, and they will not suffer from the hot or cold weather. Even though spiritual bodies cannot feel cold or hot even in cold or hot places, they can still feel the cool or warm air. So nobody will suffer from the hot or cold weather in heaven.

In fall, God's children can enjoy beautiful fallen leaves, and in winter they can see white snow. They will be able to enjoy the beauty that is much more beautiful than anything in this world. The reason God has made four seasons in heaven is to let His children know that everything they want is ready for their enjoyment in heaven. Also, it is an example of His love to satisfy His children when they miss the seasons of earth, where they were cultivated until they became God's true children.

Heaven is in the four-dimensional world that cannot be compared to this world. It is full of God's love and power, and has endless events and activities people cannot even imagine. You will learn more about the everlasting happy lives of the believers in heaven in chapter five.

Only those whose names are recorded in the Book of Life of the Lamb can enter heaven. As written in Revelation 21:6–8, only he who drinks the water of life and becomes God's child can inherit the kingdom of God:

> It is done. I am the Alpha and the Omega, the Beginning and the End. To him who is thirsty I will give to drink without cost from the spring of the water of life. He who overcomes will inherit all this, and I will be his God and he will be my son. But the cowardly, the unbelieving, the vile, the murderers, the sexually immoral, those who practice magic arts, the idolaters and all liars—their place will be in the fiery lake of burning sulfur. This is the second death.

It is an essential duty of man to fear God and keep His commandments (Ecclesiastes 12:13). So if you break His Word or do not fear God and keep on sinning even though you know you are sinning, you cannot enter heaven. Evil men, murderers, adulterers, magicians, and idol worshippers who are beyond common sense will definitely not go to heaven. They ignored God, served demons, and believed in foreign gods following the enemy Satan.

Also, those who lie to God and deceive Him and speak and blaspheme against the Holy Spirit will never enter heaven. As I explain in the book *Hell*, these people will suffer eternal punishment in hell.

Therefore, I pray in the name of the Lord that you will not only accept Jesus Christ and gain the right as a child of God but also enjoy an eternal happiness in this beautiful heaven that is as clear as crystal by following God's Word.

CHAPTER 2

THE GARDEN OF EDEN AND THE WAITING PLACE OF HEAVEN

> Now the LORD God had planted a garden in the
> east, in Eden; and there he put the man he had
> formed. And the LORD God made all kinds of trees
> grow out of the ground—trees that were pleasing
> to the eye and good for food. In the middle of
> the garden were the tree of life and the tree of the
> knowledge of good and evil.
>
> —GENESIS 2:8–9

Adam, the first man God created, lived in the Garden of Eden as a living spirit communicating with God. After a long time, however, Adam committed a sin of disobedience by eating from the tree of the knowledge of good and evil, which God had prohibited. As a result, his spirit, the master of man, died. He was driven out from the Garden of Eden and had to live on this earth. Now the spirits of Adam and Eve died and their communication with God was cut off. Living on this cursed land, how much would they have missed the Garden of Eden?

The omniscient God had known about Adam's disobedience beforehand and prepared Jesus Christ, and He opened the way of salvation when the time came. Everybody who is saved by faith will inherit heaven, which cannot be compared even to the Garden of Eden.

After Jesus' resurrection and ascension to heaven, He made a waiting place where those people who are saved can stay until the Judgment Day, preparing dwelling places for them. Let us look at the Garden of Eden and the Waiting

Place of heaven in order to better understand heaven.

THE GARDEN OF EDEN WHERE ADAM LIVED

Genesis 2:8–9 explains the Garden of Eden. This is where the first man and woman God created, Adam and Eve, used to live.

> Now the LORD God had planted a garden in the east, in Eden; and there he put the man he had formed. And the LORD God made all kinds of trees grow out of the ground—trees that were pleasing to the eye and good for food. In the middle of the garden were the tree of life and the tree of the knowledge of good and evil.

The Garden of Eden was a place where Adam, a living spirit, was going to live, so it had to be made somewhere in the spiritual world. Then, where today really is the Garden of Eden, home to the first man Adam?

The location of the Garden of Eden

God has mentioned "heaven" in many places of the Bible to let you know that there are spaces in the spiritual world beyond the sky you see with your naked eyes. He used the word *heaven* to make you understand the spaces that belong to the spiritual world.

> To the LORD your God belong the heavens, even the highest heavens, the earth and everything in it.
> —DEUTERONOMY 10:14

> But God made the earth by his power; he founded the world by his wisdom and stretched out the heavens by his understanding.
> —JEREMIAH 10:12

Praise him, you highest heavens and you waters above the
skies.

—PSALM 148:4

Therefore, you should understand that "skies" or "heavens" does not only mean the sky visible to your naked eyes. It is the First Heaven where the sun, the moon, and the stars are located, and there are the Second Heaven and the Third Heaven that belong to the spiritual world. In 2 Corinthians 12, the apostle Paul talks about the Third Heaven. The whole heaven from Paradise to New Jerusalem is in this Third Heaven.

Paul had been to Paradise, which is the place for those who have the least faith, and which is the farthest from God's throne. And there he heard about the secrets of heaven. Still, he confessed that it was "things that man is not permitted to tell" (2 Cor. 12:4)

Then, what kind of a spiritual world is the Second Heaven? This is different from the Third Heaven, and the Garden of Eden belongs here. Most people have thought that the Garden of Eden is located on this earth. Many biblical scholars and researchers continued archaeological search and studies around Mesopotamia and upper streams of the Euphrates and the Tigris in the Middle East. However, they have not uncovered anything thus far. The reason people cannot find the Garden of Eden on this earth is that it is in the Second Heaven, which belongs to the spiritual world.

The Second Heaven is also the place for the evil spirits who were driven out from the Third Heaven after the rebellion of Lucifer. Genesis 3:24 says, "After he drove the man out, he placed on the east side of the Garden of Eden cherubim and a flaming sword flashing back and forth to guard the way to the tree of life." God did this to prevent the evil spirits from gaining eternal life by entering the Garden of Eden and eating from the tree of life.

HEAVEN I

Gates to the Garden of Eden

Now you should not understand that the Second Heaven is above the First Heaven, and the Third Heaven above the Second Heaven. You cannot understand space of the four-dimensional world and above with the understanding and knowledge of the third-dimensional world. Then, how are many heavens structured? The third-dimensional world that you see and the spiritual heavens seem to be separated, but at the same time they are overlapped and connected. There are gates that connect the third-dimensional world and the spiritual world.

Although you cannot see them, gates link the First Heaven to the Garden of Eden in the Second Heaven. There are also the gates that lead to the Third Heaven. These gates are not located very high, but mainly at about the height of the clouds that you can see when you look down from inside an airplane.

In the Bible, you can realize that there are gates that go to heaven (Genesis 7:11; 2 Kings 2:11; Luke 9:28–36; Acts 1:9, 7:56). So, when the gate of heaven opens, it is possible to go up to different levels of heaven in the spiritual world, and those who are saved by faith can go up to the Third Heaven.

It is the same with Hades and hell. These places also belong to the spiritual world and there are gates that lead to these places as well. So when people with no faith die, they will go down to the Hades, which belongs to hell, or directly to hell through these gates.

The spiritual and physical dimensions coexist

The Garden of Eden, which belongs to the Second Heaven, is in the spiritual world, but it is different from the spiritual world of the Third Heaven. It is not a complete spiritual world because it can coexist with the physical world.

In other words, the Garden of Eden is a middle stage between the physical world and the spiritual world. Adam, the first man, was a living spirit, but he still had a physical body made from dust. So Adam and Eve were fruitful and increased in number there, giving birth to children the way we do (Genesis 3:16).

Even after Adam ate from the tree of the knowledge of good and evil and was driven out to this world, his children who remained in the Garden of Eden are still living to this day as living spirits, not experiencing death. The Garden of Eden is a very peaceful place where there is no death. It is run by God's power and controlled under the rules and orders that God made. Even though there is no distinction between the day and night, Adam's descendants naturally know the time to be active, the time to rest, and so forth.

Also, the Garden of Eden has very similar features as does this earth. It is filled with many plants, animals, and insects. It also has an endless and beautiful nature. Yet, there are no high mountains but only low hills. On these hills there are some house-like buildings, but people only rest—not live—in these buildings.

Vacation spot of Adam and his children

Adam lived for a very long time in the Garden of Eden, being fruitful and increasing in number. Since Adam and his children were living spirits, they could come down to this earth freely through the gates of the Second Heaven.

Because Adam and his children visited the earth as their vacation spot for a long time, you should realize that the history of mankind is very long. Some confuse this history with the six-thousand-year-old history of human cultivation and do not believe in the Bible.

If you look at the mysterious ancient civilizations carefully, however, you realize that Adam and his children used to come down to this earth. The pyramids and the Sphinx of Giza, Egypt, for instance, are also the footprints of Adam and his children who lived in the Garden of Eden. Such footprints, found throughout the world, had been constructed with much more sophisticated and advanced science and technology, after which you cannot even imitate with modern scientific knowledge today.

For example, the pyramids contain wonderful mathematical calculations, and geometrical and astronomical knowledge that you can only find and understand with advanced studies. They contain many secrets that you can fathom only when you know the exact constellations and the cycle of the universe. Some people regard those mysterious ancient civilizations as footprints of aliens from outer space, but with the Bible you can solve all the things that even science cannot understand.

The footprint of the civilization of Eden

Adam in the Garden of Eden had an unimaginable magnitude of knowledge and skill. This was the result of God having taught Adam the true knowledge, and such knowledge and understanding accumulated and developed over time. So for Adam, who knew everything about the universe and subdued the earth, it was never difficult to build the pyramids and the Sphinx. Since God had taught Adam directly, the first man knew the things that you still do not know or are able to grasp with modern science.

Some pyramids were built by Adam's skill and knowledge, others were built by his children, and still others were built by the people on this earth who tried to imitate Adam's pyramids after a long time. All these pyramids have distinct technological differences. This is because only Adam had the God-given authority to subdue all creation.

Adam lived for a very long time in the Garden of Eden, occasionally coming down to this earth, but was driven out from the Garden of Eden after committing the sin of disobedience. However, God did not close the gates that connect the earth and the Garden of Eden for some time after that.

Therefore, Adam's children who still lived in the Garden of

Eden came down to the earth freely, and as they came more often, they began to take the daughters of men as their wives (Genesis 6:1–4).

Then, God closed the gates in the sky that connect the earth with the Garden of Eden. Yet, the travel did not stop completely, but it came under strict control like never before. You must realize that most of the mysterious and unsolved ancient civilizations are footprints of Adam and his children, left during the time they could freely come down onto this earth.

History of men and dinosaurs on the earth

Why, then, is it that the dinosaurs lived on earth but suddenly became extinct? This is also one of the very important evidences that tell you how old the human history actually is. It is a secret that can only be solved with the Bible.

God had actually placed dinosaurs in the Garden of Eden. They were mild, but were driven out to this earth because they fell into the trap of Satan during the period in which Adam could freely travel back and forth between this earth and the Garden of Eden. Now, dinosaurs that were forced to live on this earth had to constantly look for things to eat. Unlike the time they lived in the Garden of Eden, where everything was abundant, this earth could not possibly produce enough food for dinosaurs with big bodies. They ate up the fruit, grains, and plants, and then began to eat up animals. They were about to destroy the environment and the food chain. God finally decided that He could no longer keep the dinosaurs on this earth, and exterminated them with fire from above.

Today, many scholars argue that dinosaurs lived on this earth for a long time. They say that dinosaurs lived for more than one hundred and sixty million years. However, none of the claims explain with satisfaction how so many dinosaurs came into being so suddenly and became extinct so suddenly. Also, if such big dinosaurs had evolved for such a long time, what would have they eaten to continue their lives?

According to the theory of evolution, before so many kinds of dinosaurs appeared, much more kinds of lower-level living creatures had to have been here, but still there is no single proof of that. Generally, for any kind of family of animal to be exterminated, it decreases in number over some time, and then disappears completely. The dinosaurs, however, disappeared suddenly.

Scholars argue that this was the result of a sudden change in weather, virus, radiation caused by the explosion of another star, or a collision of a big meteorite with the earth. Yet, if such a change had been catastrophic enough to kill all dinosaurs, all other animals and plants should have been exterminated as well. Other plants, birds, or mammals, however, are all alive even today, so the reality does not support the theory of evolution.

Even before the dinosaurs appeared on this earth, Adam and Eve lived in the Garden of Eden, sometimes coming down to earth. You should realize that the history of earth is very long.

You can learn more details from the "Lectures on Genesis" that I preached. For now, I would like to explain the beautiful nature of the Garden of Eden.

The beautiful nature of the Garden of Eden

You are lying down on your side comfortably on a plain full of fresh trees and flowers, receiving the light that softly wraps your whole body, and looking up at the blue sky where pure white clouds are floating and making various kinds of shapes.

A lake is shining beautifully down the slope, and a gentle breeze containing sweet scents of flowers passes you by swiftly. You can have delightful conversations with the ones you love, and feel happiness. Sometimes you can lie down on wide pastures or a pile of flowers and can feel the sweet scent touching the flowers gently. You can also lie down in the shadow of a tree, which is bearing many big, appetizing fruits, and eat as much as you want.

In the lake and in the sea are many kinds of colorful fish. If you want, you can go to the beach nearby and enjoy the refreshing waves or white sands that shine in the sunshine. Or, if you wish, you can even swim like the fish.

Lovely deer, rabbits, or squirrels with beautiful, shiny eyes come to you and do cute things. In the big plain, many animals are playing with each other peacefully.

This is the Garden of Eden, where there is fullness of calm, peace, and joy. Many people in this world would probably like to leave their busy lives and have this kind of peace and serenity even for once.

Abundant life in the Garden of Eden

The people in the Garden of Eden can eat and enjoy themselves as much as they want, even if they do not work for anything. There are no worries, concerns, or anxiety, and it is only full of joy, delight, and peace. Because everything is run by God's rules and orders, people there enjoy eternal life although they have not worked for anything.

In the Garden of Eden, which has a similar environment as does this earth, most features of this earth exist as well. Yet, because they do not get polluted or change from the time they were first made, they keep their clear and beautiful nature unlike their counterpart on this earth.

Genesis 3:8 notes a change in temperature in the Garden of Eden: "Then the man and his wife heard the sound of the LORD God as he was walking in the garden in the cool of the day, and they hid from the LORD God among the trees of the garden." You realize that people have "cool" feelings in the Garden of Eden. Yet, it does not mean that they have to sweat on a blazing hot day or shiver uncontrollably on a cold day as they would on this earth.

The Garden of Eden always has the most comfortable level

of temperature, humidity, and wind, so that there is no discomfort caused by changes in weather.

Also, the Garden of Eden does not have day and night. It is always surrounded with the light of God the Father, and you always feel like it is the daytime. People have time to rest, and they differentiate the time to be active from the time to rest by the change of the temperature.

This change in temperature, however, does not mean it will increase or decrease drastically to make people feel warm or cool suddenly, but it will make them feel comfortable to have rest in a gentle breeze.

PEOPLE ARE CULTIVATED ON THE EARTH

The Garden of Eden is so wide and large that you cannot possibly imagine its size. It is about a billion times as big as this earth. The First Heaven where people can only live for seventy or eighty years seems endless, stretching from our solar system to galaxies beyond. How much larger, then, would the Garden of Eden be, where people multiply in number without seeing any death, than the First Heaven?

At the same time, no matter how beautiful, abundant, and big the Garden of Eden is it can never be compared to any place in heaven. Even Paradise, which is the Waiting Place in heaven, is a much more beautiful and happier place. The eternal life in the Garden of Eden is very different from the eternal life in heaven.

Therefore, through an examination of God's plan and a number of steps on Adam's having been driven out from the Garden of Eden and cultivated on this earth, you will see how the Garden of Eden differs from the Waiting Place of heaven.

The tree of the knowledge of good and evil in the Garden of Eden

Adam could eat anything he wanted, subdue all creation,

and live eternally in the Garden of Eden. Yet, if you read Genesis 2:16–17, God commands the man, "You are free to eat from any tree in the garden; but you must not eat from the tree of the knowledge of good and evil, for when you eat of it you will surely die." Even though God had given Adam tremendous authority to subdue all creation and free will, He strictly prohibited Adam from eating from the tree of the knowledge of good and evil. In the Garden of Eden there are many kinds of colorful, beautiful, and delicious fruits that cannot be compared to the ones on this earth. God gave all the fruits under Adam's control, so he could eat them as much as he wanted.

The fruit from the tree of the knowledge of good and evil, however, was an exception. Through this you should realize that although God had already known that Adam would eat from the tree of the knowledge of good and evil, He did not just leave Adam to commit the sin. As many people misunderstand, if God had intended to test Adam by placing the tree of the knowledge of good and evil in the garden, knowing that Adam would eat of it, He would not have commanded Adam so strongly. So you see that God did not purposely place the tree of the knowledge of good and evil in the garden to let Adam eat from it or to test him.

Just as written in James 1:13, "When tempted, no one should say, 'God is tempting me.' For God cannot be tempted by evil, nor does he tempt anyone." God Himself does not test anyone.

Then, why did God place the tree of the knowledge of good and evil in the Garden of Eden?

If you can feel joyful, glad, or happy, it is because you have experienced the opposite feelings of sadness, pain, and distress. By the same token, if you know that goodness, truth, and light are good, it is because you have experienced and know that evil, untruth, and darkness are bad.

If you have not experienced this relativity, you cannot feel in your heart how good love, goodness, and happiness are even if you know in your mind from having heard of such.

For example, could a person who has never been sick or seen anybody sick know the pain of a disease? This person would not even know that it is relatively good to be healthy. Also, if a person has never been in need, and never known anyone else in need, how much would he know about poverty? This kind of person would not feel that it is "good" to be rich, no matter how rich he may be. Likewise, if one has not experienced poverty, he could not have a truly thankful mind from deep inside of his heart.

If one does not know the value of the good things he has, he does not know the value of the happiness he enjoys. However, if one has experienced the pain of disease and sorrow of poverty, he is able to be thankful in his heart for the happiness that comes from being healthy and rich. This is the reason God had to place the tree of the knowledge of good and evil in the Garden of Eden.

Therefore, Adam and Eve, who were driven out from the Garden of Eden, experienced this relativity and realized the love and blessing that God had given them. Only then could they become true children of God who knew the value of true happiness and life.

However, God did not purposely lead Adam to go that way. Adam chose to disobey God's command in his free will. In His own love and righteousness, God had planned the human cultivation.

God's providence of human cultivation

When the people of the Garden of Eden were expelled and began to be cultivated on this earth, they had to experience all kinds of sufferings such as tears, sorrow, pain, disease, and death. But it led them to feel real happiness and enjoy an eternal life in heaven, to their great gratitude.

Therefore, making us His true children through this

human cultivation is only an example of God's wonderful love and plan. Parents would not think it is a waste of time to train and sometimes punish their children if it can make a difference and make their children successful. Also, if the children believe in the glory they will receive in the future, they will be patient and overcome any difficult situations and obstacles.

Likewise, if you think of the true happiness you will enjoy in heaven, being cultivated on this earth is not something difficult or painful. Instead, you are thankful for being able to live according to God's Word because you hope for the glory you will receive later.

So whom would God consider dearer: those who are truly thankful to God after experiencing many hardships on this earth, or people in the Garden of Eden who do not really appreciate what they have even though they are living in such a beautiful and abundant environment?

God cultivated Adam, who was driven out from the Garden of Eden, and He cultivates his descendants on this earth to make them His true children. When this cultivation is over and houses are ready in heaven, the Lord will come back. If you live in heaven, you will have eternal happiness because even the lowest level of heaven cannot be compared to the beauty of the Garden of Eden.

Therefore, you should realize God's providence in the human cultivation and strive to become His true child who acts according to His Word.

THE WAITING PLACE OF HEAVEN

The descendants of Adam who disobeyed God are destined to die once, and after that to face the Great Judgment (see Hebrews 9:27). Yet, spirits of human beings are immortal, so they have to go to either heaven or hell. However, they do not go to heaven or hell directly, but stay in the Waiting Place in heaven or hell. Then what kind of place is the Waiting Place in heaven where God's children stay?

One's spirit leaves his body at the end

When a person dies, the spirit leaves the body. After death, anyone who has not known this will be very surprised when he or she sees their body lying down. Even if they are a believer, how strange will it be right after their spirit leaves their own body?

If you go to the four-dimensional world from the third-dimensional world in which you currently live, everything is very much different. The body feels very light and you feel like you are flying. Yet, you cannot have unlimited freedom even after your spirit comes out of the body.

Just as baby birds cannot fly immediately even though they are born with wings, you still need some time to adapt yourself to the spiritual world and learn the basics.

So those who die with faith in Jesus Christ are attended by two angels and go to the upper grave. There, they learn about life in heaven from the angels or prophets.

If you read the Bible, you realize that there are two kinds of graves. Forefathers of faith such as Jacob and Job said that they would go to the grave after they die. (See Genesis 37:35 and Job 7:9.) Korah and his group who opposed Moses, a man of God, fell into the grave alive. (See Numbers 16:33.)

Luke 16 portrays a rich man and a beggar named Lazarus going to the graves after they die, and you realize that they are not in the same "grave." The rich man suffers so much in the fire whereas Lazarus rests at Abraham's side far away.

Likewise, there is a grave for those who are saved whereas there is another grave for those who are not saved. The grave Korah and his men, and the rich man, ended up in is Hades, which belongs to hell, but the grave in which Lazarus ended up in is the upper grave, which belongs to heaven.

Three-day stay in the upper grave

During the time of the Old Testament, those who were saved waited in the upper grave. Since Abraham (the forefather of faith) had been in charge of the upper grave, the beggar Lazarus is at Abraham's side in Luke 16. However, since the Lord resurrected and went up to heaven, those who are saved do not go to the upper grave, to Abraham's side, anymore. They stay in the upper grave for three days and then go to somewhere in Paradise. That is, they will be with the Lord in the Waiting Place of heaven.

As Jesus says in John 14:2, "I am going there to prepare a place for you," after His resurrection and ascension to heaven, our Lord is preparing a place for each believer. Thus, since the Lord began to prepare places for God's children, those who are saved have stayed in the Waiting Place of heaven, somewhere in Paradise.

Some wonder how so many saved people since the creation can live in Paradise, but there is no need to worry. Even the solar system to which this earth belongs is only a spot compared to the galaxy. Then, how large is the galaxy? Compared to the whole universe, a galaxy is merely a spot. Then how large is the universe?

Moreover, this universe is one out of many, so it is impossible to fathom the size of the entire universe. If this physical world is so large, how much larger would the spiritual world be?

The Waiting Place of heaven

So, what kind of place is the Waiting Place of heaven where those who are saved stay after they have three days of adjusting time in the upper grave?

When people see such beautiful scenery, they utter, "This is Paradise on earth," or "It's like the Garden of Eden!" The Garden of Eden, however, cannot be compared with any beauty in this world. People in the Garden of Eden are living such wonderful, dream-like lives full of happiness, peace, and joy. Yet, it only looks good to the people on this earth. Once you go to heaven, you will immediately dismiss that notion.

Just as the Garden of Eden cannot be compared to this earth, heaven cannot be compared to the Garden of Eden. There is a fundamental difference between the happiness in the Garden of Eden that belongs to the Second Heaven, and the happiness in the Waiting Place of Paradise in the Third Heaven. This is because the people in the Garden of Eden are not really God's true children whose hearts have been cultivated.

Let me provide an example to help you understand this better. Before there was electricity, Korean ancestors used kerosene lamps. These lamps were so dark compared to the electrical lights we have today, but their light was so precious when there was no light at night. After people developed and learned to use electricity, however, we came to have electrical lights. To those who had been used to seeing only kerosene lights, electrical lights were so amazing and they were mesmerized by their brightness.

If you say that this earth is filled with complete darkness without any light, you can say the Garden of Eden is where they have kerosene lights, and heaven is a place with electrical lights. Just as kerosene light and electrical light are completely different although they are lights, the Waiting Place of heaven is completely different from the Garden of Eden.

The Waiting Place located at the edge of Paradise

The Waiting Place of heaven is located at the edge of Paradise. Paradise is the place for those who have the least faith, and it is also the farthest from the throne of God. It is a very large place.

Those who are waiting at the edge of Paradise are learning spiritual knowledge from the prophets. They learn about God the Triune, heaven, the rule of the spiritual world, etc. The extent of such knowledge is limitless, so there is no end to learning. Yet, learning spiritual things is never boring or difficult unlike some studies of this earth. The more you learn the more amazed and enlightened you become, so it is all the more graceful.

Even on this earth, those who have clean and meek hearts can communicate with God and attain spiritual knowledge. Some of these people see the spiritual world because their spiritual eyes are opened. Also, some people can realize spiritual things by the inspiration of the Holy Spirit. They can learn about faith or the rules of receiving answers to prayers, so that even in this physical world, they can experience God's power that belongs to the spirit.

If you can learn about spiritual matters and experience those things in this physical world, you will become all the more energetic and happy. Then how much more joyful and happy you would be if you could learn spiritual things in depth at the Waiting Place of heaven!

Hearing the news of this world

What kind of life do people enjoy in the Waiting Place of heaven? They experience true peace and await going to their eternal homes in heaven. They lack nothing and enjoy happiness and delight. They do not just waste time but continue to learn many things from the angels and the prophets.

Among them are designated leaders. They all live in order. They are forbidden to come down to this earth, so they are always curious about what is happening here. They are not curious about worldly things, but are curious about matters related to God's kingdom, such as "How is the church I had served doing?"; "How much of its given duty has the church accomplished?"; or "How is the world mission going?"

So they are very pleased when they hear the news about this world through the angels who can come down to this earth, or the prophets in New Jerusalem.

Heaven I

God once revealed to me about some of the members of my church who are currently staying at the Waiting Place of heaven. They are praying at separate places and waiting to hear the news about my church. They are especially interested in the duty given to my church, which is the world mission and building the Grand Sanctuary. They are very happy whenever they hear good news. So when they hear the news about the glorification of God through our overseas crusades, they get so excited and content that they have a festival.

Likewise, people in the Waiting Place of heaven are spending happy and delightful time, sometimes hearing the news about this earth.

Strict order in the Waiting Place of heaven

People of different levels of faith who will enter different places within heaven after the Judgment Day, all stay in the Waiting Place of heaven, but the orders are kept exactly. People who have less faith will show their respect to those with greater faith by bowing their heads. Spiritual orders are not decided by the position of this world, but by the extent of their sanctification and faithfulness in their God-given duties.

In this way, orders are kept strictly because the God of righteousness reigns over heaven. Since the order is decided based on the brightness of light, the extent of goodness, and the magnitude of love of each believer, nobody can complain. In heaven, everyone obeys the spiritual order because there is no evil in the minds of the saved.

However, this order and different kinds of glory are not meant to bring about forced obedience. It comes only from the love and respect from true and sincere hearts. Therefore, in the Waiting Place of heaven, they respect all those who are ahead of them in heart and show their respect by bowing their heads, because they naturally feel the spiritual difference.

PEOPLE NOT STAYING IN THE WAITING PLACE

All people who will enter respective places of heaven after the Judgment Day, are currently staying at the edge of Paradise, the Waiting Place of heaven. There are, however, some exceptions. Those who are to go to New Jerusalem, the most beautiful place in heaven, will go straight into New Jerusalem and help with God's work. These people, who have the heart of God that is clear and beautiful as crystal, are living in God's special love and care.

They will help with God's work in New Jerusalem

Where would our forefathers of faith, sanctified and faithful in all God's house, such as Elijah, Enoch, Abraham, Moses, and the apostle Paul, be staying now? Are they staying at the edge of Paradise, the Waiting Place of heaven? No. Because these people are completely sanctified and resemble God's heart fully, they are already in New Jerusalem. Yet, because the judgment has not yet taken place, they cannot go into their would-be respective, eternal houses.

Then, where in New Jerusalem are they staying? In New Jerusalem, which has fifteen hundred miles of width, length, and height, there are a couple of spiritual spaces of different dimensions. There is a place for God's throne, some places where houses are being built, and other places where our forefathers of faith who have already entered New Jerusalem are working with the Lord.

Our forefathers of faith staying already in New Jerusalem are longing for the day when they will enter their eternal places, while helping with God's work with the Lord in preparation of our places. They are longing very much to enter their eternal houses because they can enter there only after Jesus Christ's Second Advent in the air, the Seven-Year Wedding Banquet, and the Millennium on this earth.

The apostle Paul, who was full of a hope for heaven, confessed the following in 2 Timothy 4:7–8:

> I have fought the good fight, I have finished the race, I have kept the faith. Now there is in store for me the crown of righteousness, which the Lord, the righteous Judge, will award to me on that day—and not only to me, but also to all who have longed for his appearing.

Those who are fighting the good fight and hoping for the Lord's return have a definite hope for the place and rewards in heaven. This kind of faith and hope can increase if you know more about the spiritual realm, and that is why I am explaining heaven in detail.

The Garden of Eden in the Second Heaven or the Waiting Place in the Third Heaven is still more beautiful than this world, but even these places cannot be compared to the glory and splendor of New Jerusalem which houses God's throne.

Therefore, I pray in the name of the Lord that you will not only run toward New Jerusalem with the sort of faith and hope of the apostle Paul, but also lead many souls to the way of salvation by spreading the gospel, even if that task demands your life.

CHAPTER 3

THE SEVEN-YEAR WEDDING BANQUET

> Blessed and holy are those who have part in the
> first resurrection. The second death has no power
> over them, but they will be priests of God and
> of Christ and will reign with him for a thousand
> years.
>
> —REVELATION 20:6

Before you receive your reward and begin an eternal life in heaven, you go through the judgment of the White Throne. Before the day of Great Judgment, there will be the Lord's Second Advent in the air, the Seven-Year Wedding Banquet, the Lord's coming back to the earth, and the Millennium.

All this is what God has prepared to comfort His beloved children who kept their faith on this earth, and to allow them to have a taste of heaven.

Therefore, those who believe in the Second Advent of the Lord and hope to meet Him, who is our bridegroom, will look forward to the Seven-Year Wedding Banquet and the Millennium. The Word of God recorded in the Bible is true and all the prophecies are being accomplished today.

You should be a wise believer and try your best to prepare yourself as His bride, realizing that if you are not awake and do not live according to God's Word, the day of the Lord will come like a thief and you will fall into death.

Let us look in detail at the wondrous things that the children of God will experience before they go into heaven, which is clear and beautiful as crystal.

JESUS' RETURN AND THE SEVEN-YEAR WEDDING BANQUET

The apostle Paul writes in Romans 10:9: "That if you confess with your mouth, 'Jesus is Lord,' and believe in your heart that God raised him from the dead, you will be saved." In order to gain salvation, you must not only confess Jesus as your Savior but also believe in your heart that He died and rose again from the dead.

If you do not believe in Jesus' resurrection, you cannot believe in your own would-be resurrection at the Second Coming of the Lord. You will not even be able to believe in the Lord's return. If you cannot believe in the existence of heaven and hell, then you will not gain the strength to live according to God's Word, and you will not gain salvation.

The ultimate goal of Christian life

It says in 1 Corinthians 15:19, "If only for this life we have hope in Christ, we are to be pitied more than all men." The children of God, unlike unbelievers of the world, come to church, attend the services, and serve the Lord in many ways every Sunday. In order to live according to God's Word, they often fast, and pray earnestly at the sanctuary of God in the early morning or late at night even though they would some-times need a rest.

Also, they do not seek their own benefits, but serve others and sacrifice themselves for the kingdom of God. That is why if there was no heaven, the faithful are to be pitied the most. Yet, it is certain that the Lord is coming back to take you to heaven, and He is preparing a beautiful place for you. He will reward you according to what you have sown and done in this world.

Jesus says in Matthew 16:27, "For the Son of Man is going to come in his Father's glory with his angels, and then he will reward each person according to what he has done." Here, to "reward according to what he has done" does not simply mean going to either heaven or hell. Even among the believers who go to heaven, the reward and glory given to them are different according to how they lived in this world.

Some resent and fear to hear that the Lord is coming back soon. Yet, if you truly love the Lord and hope for heaven, it is natural that you long and wait to meet the Lord sooner. If you confess with your lips, "I love you, Lord," but dislike and even fear to hear that the Lord is coming back soon, it cannot be said that you really love the Lord.

Therefore, you should receive the Lord your bridegroom with joy by looking forward to His Second Coming in your heart and preparing yourself as a bride.

The Lord's Second Advent in the air

It is written in 1 Thessalonians 4:16–17, "For the Lord himself will come down from heaven, with a loud command, with the voice of the archangel and with the trumpet call of God, and the dead in Christ will rise first. After that, we who are still alive and are left will be caught up together with them in the clouds to meet the Lord in the air. And so we will be with the Lord forever."

When the Lord comes back again in the air, each child of God will change into a spiritual body and be caught up in the air to receive the Lord. There are some people who have been saved and died. Their bodies are buried but their spirits are waiting in Paradise. We refer to such people as being "asleep in the Lord." Their spirits will combine with their spiritual bodies that were transformed from their old, buried bodies. They will be followed by those who will receive the Lord without seeing death, change to spiritual bodies, and be caught up in the air.

God gives a wedding banquet in the air

When the Lord returns in the air, everyone who has been

saved from the time of the creation will receive the Lord as the bridegroom. At this time, God commences the Seven-Year Wedding Banquet to comfort His children who been saved through faith. They will certainly receive the rewards in heaven for their deeds later on, but for now God still gives this banquet in the air to comfort all His children.

For example, if a general returns in a great triumph, what will the king do? He will give the general many kinds of rewards for distinguished services. The king may give him a house, land, monetary reward, and also a party to compensate for his services.

By the same token, God gives His children the place to stay and rewards in heaven after the day of Great Judgment, but before that He also gives a Wedding Banquet to let His children have a good time and share their joy. Although what everybody has done for the kingdom of God in this world is different, He gives the banquet even for the fact that they have been saved.

Then, where is the "air" in which the Seven-Year Wedding Banquet will be held? The "air" here does not refer to the sky visible to your naked eyes. If this "air" were just the sky you see with your eyes, all those who are saved must have the banquet floating in the sky. Also, there must be so many people who are saved since the creation, and all of them could not stay in this sky of the earth.

Moreover, the banquet will have been planned and prepared very well in detail because God Himself will provide it to comfort His children. There is a place that God has provided for a long time. This place is the "air" that God prepared for the Seven-Year Wedding Banquet, and this space is in the Second Heaven.

"Air" belongs to the Second Heaven

Ephesians 2:2 speaks of the time "in which you used to live when you followed the ways of this world and of the ruler of the kingdom of the air, the spirit who is now at work in those who are disobedient." So the "air" is also a place where the evil spirits have authority.

However, the place where there will be the Seven-Year Wedding Banquet and the place where evil spirits exist are not the same. The reason the same expression "air" is used is because both of them belong to the Second Heaven. Yet, even the Second Heaven is not one single space, but is divided into different areas. So the place where the Wedding Banquet will be held and the place where the evil spirits exist are separated.

God made a new spiritual realm called the Second Heaven by taking some portion of the whole spiritual realm. Then He divided it into two areas. One is Eden, which is the area of the light belonging to God, and the other is the area of darkness that God has given to the evil spirits.

God made the Garden of Eden, where Adam would stay until the human cultivation began, in the east of Eden. God took Adam and put him in this Garden. Also, God has given the area of darkness to the evil spirits and allowed them to stay there. This area of darkness and Eden are strictly divided.

Place of the Seven-Year Wedding Banquet

Then, where will the Seven-Year Wedding Banquet be held? The Garden of Eden is only a part of Eden, and there are many other spaces in Eden. In one of those spaces God has provided a space for the Seven-Year Wedding Banquet.

The place where the Seven-Year Wedding Banquet will be held is much more beautiful than the Garden of Eden. There are such beautiful flowers and trees. Lights of many colors shine brightly, and an inexpressibly beautiful and clean nature surrounds the place.

Also, it is so vast because all those who have been saved since the creation will have the banquet together. There is a very big castle that is large enough for everybody invited to the banquet to enter. The banquet will be held in this castle, and there will be unimaginably happy moments. Now, I would like to invite you to the castle for the Seven-Year Wedding Banquet. I hope you can feel the happiness of being a bride of the Lord. Who is the guest of honor of the banquet?

Meeting the Lord in a bright and beautiful place

When you arrive at the banquet hall, you will find such a brilliant room filled with the brightest lights you have ever seen. You will feel as if your body is lighter than feathers. When you softly land on the green grass, the surroundings that are not visible at first because of the terribly bright lights will begin to be seen by your eyes. You will see a sky and a lake clear and pure that dazzles your eyes. This lake shines like jewels radiating their beautiful colors whenever the water ripples.

All four sides are full of flowers, and green woods surround the entire area. Flowers swing back and forth as if they were waving to you. You can smell such thick, beautiful, and sweet scents you have never smelled before. Soon birds of many colors come and welcome you with their singing. The lake is so clear that you can see things beneath the surface. Marvelously beautiful fish stick out their heads and welcome you.

Even the grass on which you stand is as soft as cotton. The wind that makes your clothes gently flutter wraps you softly. At that moment, a strong light comes into your eyes and you see one person standing in the midst of that light.

The Lord hugs you, saying, "My bride, I love you."

With a gentle smile on His face, He calls you to come toward Him with His arms wide open. When you go up to Him, His face becomes clearly visible. You see His face for the first time, but you know very well who He is. He is the Lord Jesus, your Bridegroom, whom you love and have been longing to see all this time. At this moment, tears start flowing down your cheeks. You cannot stop shedding your tears because you are reminded of the times you were being cultivated on this earth.

You are seeing the Lord face-to-face now through whom you could prevail in the world even in the most difficult situations and when you met many persecutions and trials. The Lord comes to you, embraces you in His bosom, and tells you, "My bride, I have been waiting for this day. I love you."

Upon hearing this, even more tears pour down. Then the Lord gently wipes your tears and holds you tighter. When you look into His eyes, you can feel His heart. "I know all about you. I know all your tears and pains. There will only be happiness and joy."

For how long have you been longing for this moment? When you are in His arms, you are at utmost peace, and joy and abundance wrap your whole body.

Now, you can hear a soft, deep, and beautiful sound of praise. Then, the Lord holds your hand and leads you to the place which the praise is coming from.

The wedding banquet hall is full of colorful lights

A moment later, you see a splendid, shining castle that is so magnificent and beautiful. When you stand in front of the gate of the castle, it opens gently and the bright lights from the castle come out. When you go into the castle with the Lord as if you were drawn to the inside by the light, there is such a large hall that you cannot see the other end of it. The hall is decorated with beautiful ornaments and objects, and is full of colorful and bright lights.

The sound of praises has become clearer by now, and it goes all around the hall softly. Finally, the Lord announces the beginning of the wedding banquet with a resounding voice. The Seven-Year Wedding Banquet begins, and it feels like the event is taking place in your dreams.

Do you feel the happiness of this moment? Of course, not everybody who is at the banquet can be with the Lord like this. Only those who have the qualifications can follow Him closely and be embraced by Him.

Therefore, you should prepare yourself as a bride and participate in the divine nature. Yet, even if all of the people cannot hold the Lord's hand, they will feel the same happiness and fullness.

Enjoying happy moments with singing and dancing

Once the wedding banquet begins, you sing and dance with the Lord, celebrating the name of God the Father. You dance with the Lord, talk about the times on this earth, or about heaven in which you are going to live.

You also talk about the love of God the Father and glorify Him. You can have wonderful conversations with the people with whom you have wanted to be for a long time.

As you enjoy the fruit that melt in your mouth, and drink the Water of Life that flows from the Father's throne, the banquet continues sweetly. You do not, however, have to stay in the castle for the entire span of seven years. From time to time, you go out of the castle and spend joyful moments.

Then, what are some happy activities and events that await you outside the castle? You can have time to enjoy the beautiful nature making friends with woods, trees, flowers, and birds. You can walk with your beloved people on the roads decorated with such beautiful flowers, talk with them, or sometimes praise the Lord with singing and dancing. Also, there are many things you can enjoy in big open places. For example, people can go boating on the lake with beloved ones or with the Lord Himself. You can go swimming or enjoy many kinds of entertainment and games. Many things that give you unimaginable joy and delight are provided by God's detailed care and love.

During the seven years of the wedding banquet no light is ever turned off. Of course, Eden is an area of light and there is no night there. In Eden, you do not have to go to sleep and take a rest as you do on this earth. No matter how long you enjoy, you never grow tired, and instead you become more delighted and happy.

This is why you do not feel the flow of time, and the seven years passes like seven days, or even seven hours. Even if there are your parents, children, or siblings who had not been lifted and are suffering from the Great Tribulation, time goes so fast with joy and happiness that you cannot even think of them.

Giving more thanks for being saved

The people of the Garden of Eden and the wedding banquet guests can see each other, but they cannot come and go. Also, the evil spirits can see the wedding banquet and you can see them as well. Of course, the evil ones cannot even think of approaching the banquet place, but you can still see them. Seeing the banquet and the happiness of the guests, the evil spirits suffer a great pain. For them, not having been able to take one more person to hell and giving people up to God as His children is an unbearable pain.

Conversely, by looking at the evil spirits, you are reminded of how much they have tried to devour you like a roaring lion while you were being cultivated on this earth.

Then, you become even more thankful for the grace of God the Father, the Lord, and the Holy Spirit who protected you from the power of darkness and led you to become a child of God. Also, you become more thankful to those who helped you go to the way of life.

So the Seven-Year Wedding Banquet is not only a time to rest and be comforted for the pain of having been cultivated on this earth, but also a time to be reminded of the times on this earth and be more thankful for the love of God.

You also think about the eternal life in heaven that will be much more delightful than the Seven-Year Wedding Banquet. The happiness in heaven cannot be compared to that of the Seven-Year Wedding Banquet.

The Seven-Year Great Tribulation

While the happy wedding banquet is being held in the air, the Seven-Year Great Tribulation takes place on this earth. Due to the kind and magnitude of the Great Tribulation that has never been and never will be, much of the earth is destroyed and most of the people who are left die.

Of course, some of them are saved by what is called the "gleaning salvation." There are many who are left on this earth after the Second Advent of the Lord because they did not believe at all, or did not believe properly. Yet, when they repent during the Seven-Year Great Tribulation and become martyrs, they can be saved. This is called the "gleaning salvation."

Becoming a martyr during the Seven-Year Great Tribulation, however, is not easy. Even if they decide to become a martyr in the beginning, most of them end up denying the Lord because of cruel tortures and persecutions given by the Antichrist who forces them to receive the "666" mark of the beast (Rev. 13:17). They usually strongly refuse to receive the sign because once received, they know they would belong to Satan. Yet, it is anything but easy at all to bear the tortures accompanied by extreme pains.

Sometimes even if one can overcome the tortures, it is even more difficult to watch his beloved family members being tortured. That is why it is very hard to be saved by this "gleaning salvation." Moreover, because people cannot receive any help from the Holy Spirit during this time, it is even more difficult to maintain the faith.

Therefore, I hope that none of the readers will face the Seven-Year Great Tribulation. The reason why I explain about the Seven-Year Great Tribulation is to let you know that the events recorded in the Bible about the end of time are being and will be accomplished precisely.

Another reason is also for those who will be left on the earth after God's children have been caught up in the air.

While true believers go up to the air and have the Seven-Year Wedding Banquet, the miserable Seven-Year Great Tribulation takes place on this earth.

Martyrs gain "gleaning salvation"

After the Lord's return in the air, there will be some who repent of their improper faith in Jesus Christ among the people who are not lifted up to the air.

What leads them to the "gleaning salvation" is the Word of God preached by the church that shows God's works of power greatly at the end of time. They come to know how to be saved, what kind of events will unfold, and how they should react to the world events prophesied through the Word of God.

So there are some people who really repent before God and are saved by becoming martyrs. It is so-called "gleaning salvation." Of course, among such people are Israelis. They will come to know about "the message of the Cross" and realize Jesus, whom they did not recognize as the Messiah, is truly the Son of God and the Savior for all mankind. Then they will repent and be a part of the "gleaning salvation." They will gather to grow their faith together, and some of them will become aware of the heart of God and become martyrs to be saved.

In this way, writings that explain God's Word clearly are not only helpful to increase many believers' faith, but they also play a very important role for those who are not caught up in the air. Therefore, you should realize the wondrous love and mercy of God, who has provided everything for those who will be saved even after the Lord's Second Advent in the air.

THE MILLENNIUM

The brides who have finished the Seven-Year Wedding Banquet will come down to this earth and reign with the Lord for a thousand years. (See Revelation 20:4.) When the Lord comes back to the earth, He will clean it up. He will clear first the air and then make all the nature beautiful.

Visiting all around the newly cleansed earth

Just as a newly married couple goes on a honeymoon, you will go on trips with the Lord your Bridegroom during the Millennium after the Seven-Year Wedding Banquet. Where, then, will you want to visit the most?

God's children, the brides of the Lord, would want to visit this earth here and there since they will have to leave it soon. God will move all the things in the First Heaven, such as the earth on which human cultivation took place, the sun, and the moon to another space after the Millennium.

Therefore, after the Seven-Year Wedding Banquet, God the Father will refurnish the earth beautifully and let you reign over it with the Lord for one thousand years before He moves it away. This is a pre-planned process within the providence of God that He created all things in heaven and earth for six days, and rested on the seventh day. Letting you reign on the earth with the Lord for one thousand years is also so you do not to feel sorry for leaving the earth. You will enjoy the delightful time reigning with the Lord for one thousand years on this beautifully refurnished earth. Visiting all the places that you have not been while you were living on this earth, you can feel the happiness and joy that you have not felt before.

Reigning one thousand years

During this time, there is no enemy, no Satan. Just like in the Garden of Eden, there will only be peace and rest in such comfortable environments. Also, the Lord and those who are saved will stay on this earth, but they will not live with the fleshly people who survived the Great Tribulation. The saved people and the Lord will live in a separated place, like a royal palace or castle. In other words, spiritual ones will live within the castle and the fleshly ones outside the castle because the spiritual and fleshly bodies cannot stay together in one place.

Spiritual people will have already changed into spiritual bodies and have eternal life. So they can smell aromas like the scent of flowers, but do not have to eat. However, they can eat with fleshly people when they are together. Yet, even if they eat, they do not excrete like the fleshly people. Even if they eat physical food, they dissolve it into the air through their breath.

Fleshly people will concentrate on increasing their number because there are not many survivors from the Seven-Year Great Tribulation. At this time, there will be no diseases or evil because the air is clean, and the enemy, Satan, will not be there. This is because the Satan and the devils that control the evilness are imprisoned in the bottomless pit, or the abyss. The unrighteousness and the evil in the human nature will not exert influence. (See Revelation 20:3.) Also, since there is no death, the earth will be filled with many people again.

Then, what will the fleshly people eat? When Adam and Eve lived in the Garden of Eden, they ate only fruits and seed-bearing plants. (See Genesis 1:29.) After Adam and Eve disobeyed God and were driven out from the Garden of Eden, they began to eat the plants of the field. (See Genesis 3:18.) After the flood of Noah's time, the world became more evil and God permitted mankind to eat meat. You see the more evil the world became, the more evil the food people ate became.

During the Millennium, people eat crops of the field or fruits of the trees. They will not eat any meat, just as the people before the flood of Noah did, because there will be no evil or killing. Also, because all civilizations will have been destroyed by wars during the Great Tribulation, they will return to the primitive way of life and increase in number on the earth, which the Lord refurnished. They will start anew in the pure nature, which is unpolluted, peaceful, and beautiful.

Furthermore, even though they had experienced such a developed civilization before the Great Tribulation and had knowledge, today's modern civilization cannot be accomplished within one or two hundred years. Yet, as the time passes and people gather their wisdom, they may be able to accomplish a civilization of today's level at the end of the Millennium.

HEAVEN REWARDED AFTER THE JUDGMENT DAY

After the Millennium, God will set Satan free from the abyss (the bottomless pit) for a short time. (See Revelation 20:1–3.) Although the Lord Himself reigns on this earth to lead the fleshly people who survive the Great Tribulation and their descendants to eternal salvation, their faith is not true. So, God lets the enemy Satan tempt them.

Many of the fleshly people will be deceived by the enemy devil and go to the way of destruction. (See Revelation 20:8.) The people of God will again realize the reason God had to make hell, and they will realize the great love of God who wants to gain true children through human cultivation.

The evil spirits that are set free for a short time will again be put in the bottomless pit, and the Great Judgment of the White Throne will take place. (See Revelation 20:10–12.) Then, how will the Great Judgment of the White Throne be done?

God presides over the judgment of the White Throne

In July 1982, while I was praying for the opening of a church, I came to know about the Great Judgment of the White Throne in detail. God revealed to me a scene in which God judges everybody. In front of the throne of God the Father stood the Lord and Moses, and around the throne were people playing the role of a jury.

Unlike judges of this world, God is perfect and makes no mistakes. Yet, He still judges along with the Lord who serves as the advocate of love, Moses as the prosecutor with the law, and other people as jury members. Revelation 20:11–15 describes exactly how God will judge:

> Then I saw a great white throne and him who was seated on it. Earth and sky fled from his presence, and there was no place for them. And I saw the dead, great and small, standing before the throne, and books were opened. Another book was opened, which is the book of life. The dead were judged according to what they had done as recorded in the books. The sea gave up the dead that were in it, and death and Hades gave up the dead that were in them, and each person was judged according to what he had done. Then death and Hades were thrown into the lake of fire. The lake of fire is the second death. If anyone's name was not found written in the book of life, he was thrown into the lake of fire.

"The great white throne" here refers to the throne of God, who is the judge. God, seated on the throne that is as bright as to look "white," will perform the final judgment with love and righteousness to send the chaff, not the wheat, to hell.

That is why it is sometimes called the Great Judgment of the White Throne. God will judge exactly according to the Book of Life, which had recorded the names of those who are saved, and other books that record the acts of each person.

The unsaved will fall into hell

In front of the throne of God there is not only the Book of Life but also other books that record all the deeds of each person who did not accept the Lord or who did not have true faith. (See Revelation 20:12.)

From the moment people were born to the moment the Lord called their spirits, every single act is recorded in these books. For example, performing good deeds, swearing at somebody, hitting somebody, or getting angry with people are all recorded by the hands of the angels.

Just as you can record and preserve certain conversations or events for a long time through video or audio recording, the angels write down and record all situations in the books in heaven by the command of the almighty God. Therefore, the Great Judgment of the White Throne will take place exactly without any mistake. How, then, will the judgment be carried out?

The unsaved people will be judged first. These people cannot come before God to be judged because they are sinners. They will only be judged in Hades, the Waiting Place of hell. Even though they do not come before God, the judgment will be carried out just as strictly as if it were taking place in front of God Himself.

Among the sinners, God will first judge the ones whose sins are heavier. After the judgment of all those who are not saved, they will all go into either the lake of fire or the lake of burning sulfur and be punished eternally.

The saved receive rewards in heaven

After the judgment of those who are not saved is completed in such a manner, the judgment of the rewards of those who are saved will follow. As it is promised in Revelation 22:12: "Behold, I am coming soon! My reward is with me, and I will give to everyone according to what he has done," the places and rewards in heaven will be determined accordingly.

The judgment for the rewards will take place in peace in front of God because it is for the children of God. The judgment for rewards proceeds from starting with the ones who have the greatest and most rewards to the ones with least rewards, and then the children of God will enter their respective places.

There will be no more night. They will not need the light of a lamp or the light of the sun, for the Lord God will give them light. And they will reign for ever and ever.

—Revelation 22:5

Despite many hardships and difficulties in this world, how happy it is because you have the hope of heaven! There you live with the Lord forever with only happiness and delight, with no tears, sorrow, pain, disease, or death.

I have described only a little bit about the Seven-Year Wedding Banquet and the Millennium during which you will reign with the Lord. When these times, which are only a prelude to life in heaven, are so happy, how happier and more joyful will life be in heaven? Therefore, you should run toward your place and rewards prepared for you in heaven until the moment the Lord comes back to take you.

Why have our forefathers of faith tried so hard and suffered so much to take the narrow way of the Lord, instead of the easy way of this world? They fasted and prayed many nights to cast away their sins and dedicate themselves completely because they had the hope for heaven. Because they believed in God who would reward them in heaven according to their deeds, they tried so vigorously to become holy and be faithful in all God's house.

Therefore, I pray in the name of the Lord that you will not only participate in the Seven-Year Wedding Banquet and be in the Lord's arms, but also stay close to the throne of God in heaven by trying your very best with a fervent hope for heaven.

CHAPTER 4
SECRETS OF HEAVEN HIDDEN SINCE THE CREATION

He replied, "The knowledge of the secrets of the kingdom of heaven has been given to you, but not to them. Whoever has will be given more, and he will have an abundance. Whoever does not have, even what he has will be taken from him....Jesus spoke all these things to the crowd in parables; he did not say anything to them without using a parable. So was fulfilled what was spoken through the prophet: "I will open my mouth in parables, I will utter things hidden since the creation of the world."

—MATTHEW 13:11–12, 34–35

One day, when Jesus sat on the seashore, many people gathered. Then Jesus told them many things in parables. Jesus' disciples asked Him at this time.

"Why do you speak to the people in parables?"

"The knowledge of the secrets of the kingdom of heaven has been given to you, but not to them. Whoever has will be given more, and he will have an abundance. Whoever does not have, even what he has will be taken from him... But blessed are your eyes because they see, and your ears because they hear. For I tell you the truth, many prophets and righteous men longed to see what you see but did not see it, and to hear what you hear but did not hear it." (See Matthew 13:10–17.)

Just as Jesus said, many prophets and the righteous could not see or hear the secrets of the kingdom of heaven although they wanted to see and hear them. Yet, because

Jesus, who is God Himself in the very nature, came down onto this earth (Phil. 2:6–8), it was allowed for the secrets of heaven to be revealed to His disciples.

As it is written in Matthew 13:35: "So was fulfilled what was spoken through the prophet: 'I will open my mouth in parables, I will utter things hidden since the creation of the world,'" Jesus spoke in parables to fulfill what was written in the Scriptures.

SECRETS OF HEAVEN HAVE BEEN REVEALED SINCE JESUS' TIME

"The way of the Cross," which is the way to become true children of God, was planned even before the creation, but had been hidden in secret. (See 1 Corinthians 2:7.) If it had not been hidden, the enemy Satan would not have crucified Jesus, and the way for human salvation would not have been opened.

In the same way, had the secrets of heaven not been hidden since the time of the Creation, the human cultivation to gain true children of God would not have taken place. However, after Jesus came to this earth and began His ministry, He allowed the secrets of heaven to be known because He wanted people to bear abundant fruits by understanding them.

Jesus reveals secrets of heaven through parables

In Matthew 13 there are many parables about heaven. This is because without parables, you cannot understand and realize the secrets of heaven even if you read the Bible many times.

> The kingdom of heaven is like a man who sowed good seed in his field (v. 24).

> The kingdom of heaven is like a mustard seed, which a

man took and planted in his field. Though it is the smallest of all your seeds, yet when it grows... (vv. 31–32).

The kingdom of heaven is like yeast that a woman took and mixed into a large amount of flour until it worked all through the dough (v. 33).

The kingdom of heaven is like treasure hidden in a field (v. 44).

The kingdom of heaven is like a merchant looking for fine pearls (v. 45).

The kingdom of heaven is like a net that was let down into the lake and caught all kinds of fish (v. 47).

Likewise, Jesus preached about heaven, which is in the spiritual realm, through many parables. Because heaven is in the invisible spiritual realm, you can grasp it only through parables.

In order to have eternal life in heaven, you must live a proper life of faith knowing how to possess heaven, what kind of people will enter there, and when it will come to be fulfilled.

What is the ultimate goal of going to church and living a life of faith? It is to be saved and go to heaven. Yet, if you can't go to heaven although you have attended church for a long time, how pitiful will you be?

Even during the time of Jesus, many people obeyed the law and professed their belief in God, but were not qualified to be saved and enter heaven. In Matthew 3, for this reason, John the Baptist proclaims, "Repent, for the kingdom of heaven is near" (v. 2), and he prepared the way of the Lord. Also, he told people that Jesus is the Savior and the Lord of the Great Judgment, saying, "I baptize you with water for repentance. But after me will come one...He will baptize you with the

Holy Spirit and with fire. His winnowing fork is in his hand, and he will clear his threshing floor, gathering his wheat into the barn and burning up the chaff with unquenchable fire" (vv. 11–12).

Nevertheless, the Israelites of the time not only failed to recognize Him as their Savior but also crucified Him. How sad it is that they still await the Messiah even today!

The secrets of heaven revealed to the apostle Paul

Although the apostle Paul was not one of Jesus' original twelve disciples, he was not behind anybody in testifying about Jesus Christ. Before Paul met the Lord, he had been a Pharisee who had strictly kept the law and the tradition of the elders. He was also a Jew holding Roman citizenship since birth, who took part in persecuting early Christians.

However, after meeting the Lord on his way to Damascus, Paul changed his mind and led so many people to the way of salvation by concentrating on the evangelization of the Gentiles. (See Acts 9.)

God knew that Paul would suffer from so much pain and persecution while preaching the gospel. That is why He revealed the wondrous secrets of heaven to Paul so that he would run toward the goal (See Philippians 3:12–14.) God let him preach the gospel with utmost gladness with the hope of heaven.

If you read the Epistles of Paul, you can see that his writings are full of the inspiration of the Holy Spirit about the Lord's coming back, believers' being caught up in the air, their dwelling places in heaven, the glory of heaven, eternal rewards and crowns, Melchizedek the everlasting priest, and Jesus Christ.

In 2 Corinthians 12, Paul shares his spiritual experiences with the church in Corinth that he had founded, which was not living according to God's Word.

I must go on boasting. Although there is nothing to be

gained, I will go on to visions and revelations from the Lord. I know a man in Christ who fourteen years ago was caught up to the third heaven. Whether it was in the body or out of the body I do not know—God knows. And I know that this man—whether in the body or apart from the body I do not know, but God knows—was caught up to paradise. He heard inexpressible things, things that man is not permitted to tell.

—2 CORINTHIANS 12:1–4

God selected the apostle Paul for the evangelization of the Gentiles, refined him with fire, and gave him visions and revelations. God led him to overcome all hardships with love, faith, and hope for heaven. For instance, Paul confessed that he had been led to Paradise in the Third Heaven and heard about the secrets of heaven fourteen years prior, but they were so wondrous that he was not permitted to tell.

An apostle is a person who is called by God and completely obeys His will. Nevertheless, there were some people among the members of the Corinthian church who were deceived by false teachers and judged the apostle Paul.

At this time, the apostle Paul listed the hardships he had suffered for the Lord and shared his spiritual experiences in an effort to lead Corinthians to become beautiful brides of the Lord, acting according to God's Word. This was not to boast of his spiritual experiences, but only to build up and strengthen the church of Christ by defending and confirming his apostleship.

What you have to realize here is that the visions and revelations of the Lord can only be given to those who are proper in the eyes of God. Also, unlike members of the Corinthian church who were deceived by false teachers and judged Paul, you must not judge anybody who works to expand the kingdom of God, saves many people, and is recognized by God.

HEAVEN I

The secrets of heaven shown to the apostle John

The apostle John was one of the twelve disciples and was loved by Jesus very much. Jesus Himself had not only called him a "disciple" but also nurtured him spiritually so that he could serve his teacher from a close distance. He had been so short-tempered that he used to be called a "son of thunder," but he became an apostle of love after being transformed by the power of God. John followed Jesus, seeking the glory in heaven. He was also the only disciple who heard the last seven words Jesus spoke on the cross. He was faithful in his duty as an apostle, and became a great man in heaven.

As a result of severe persecution of Christianity by the Roman Empire, John was thrown into boiling oil, but he did not die. He was then exiled to the island of Patmos. There he communicated with God in depth and recorded the Book of Revelation, which is full of the secrets of heaven.

John wrote on so many spiritual things such as the throne of God and of the Lamb in heaven, worshiping in heaven, the four living creatures around God's throne, the Seven Years of the Great Tribulation and the role of angels, the Wedding Banquet of the Lamb and the Millennium, the Great Judgment of the White Throne, hell, New Jerusalem in heaven, and the bottomless pit, the abyss.

That is why the apostle John says that the Book of Revelation is recorded through the revelations and the visions of the Lord, and he is writing everything down because everything written will take place soon.

> The revelation of Jesus Christ, which God gave him to show his servants what must soon take place. He made it known by sending his angel to his servant John, who testifies to everything he saw—that is, the word of God and the testimony of Jesus Christ. Blessed is the one who reads the words of this prophecy, and blessed are those who hear

it and take to heart what is written in it, because the time
is near.

—REVELATION 1:1–3

The phrase "the time is near" implies that the time of the
Lord's return is near. Therefore, it is very important to have
the qualifications to enter heaven by being saved with faith.

Even if you go to church every week, you cannot be saved
unless you have faith with deeds. Jesus tells us, "Not everyone who says to me, 'Lord, Lord,' will enter the kingdom of
heaven, but only he who does the will of my Father who is in
heaven" (Matt. 7:21). So if you do not act according to God's
Word, it is obvious that you cannot enter heaven.

Therefore, in Revelation 4–22 the apostle John explains in
detail the events and prophecies that will take place and soon
be fulfilled. He concludes that the Lord is coming back and
you have to wash your robe. Spiritually, a robe stands for one's
heart and action. Washing the robe refers to repenting of the
sins and trying to live according to God's will.

> Behold, I am coming soon! My reward is with me, and
> I will give to everyone according to what he has done. I
> am the Alpha and the Omega, the First and the Last, the
> Beginning and the End. Blessed are those who wash their
> robes, that they may have the right to the tree of life and
> may go through the gates into the city.

—REVELATION 22:12–14

So to the extent to which you live according to God's Word,
you will pass the gates until you enter the most beautiful of
heaven, New Jerusalem.

In my book *The Measure of Faith* that will be published a
little while later, it is explained that even faith has a process
of growth. Likewise, the apostle John classified faith into the

faith of the little children, children, young men, and fathers. Therefore, you should realize that the more your faith grows, the better your dwelling place in heaven will be.

Secrets of heaven are revealed even today

About 1,900 years have passed since the apostle John recorded the Book of Revelation. Today, the time of the Lord's return is much nearer than it was then. That is why God opens the spiritual eyes of some people and allows them to see heaven and hell. He allows the spirits of some to visit heaven and hell for a certain amount of time, and encourages them to spread what they witnessed to both believers and nonbelievers.

I feel sorry for not being able to explain a great deal about heaven and hell because they belong to such a big spiritual realm. Sometimes people deliver the message incorrectly, or the listeners do not understand it altogether.

I also longed to know about heaven so much, and I received the answer and came to know the secrets of heaven in detail after I prayed and fasted many times for seven years. In May of 1984, just before my birthday, God ordered me to fast for three days in my prayer place, which was very far away from my church members. He let me have deep communications with Him. He explained heaven in detail at that time, and it took about 120 pages worth of notes on college notebooks. He explained the wondrous, amazing, and happy life of heaven, and different dwelling places and rewards people will receive according to the measure of their faith. At one point during my ministry, I preached about heaven for several months.

Afterward, God further revealed the secrets of heaven as He explained the Book of Revelation, and He continued to explain those things in greater depth after 1998. God has been revealing so many things hidden since before the beginning of time, and just as the apostle Paul confessed of "things that man is not permitted to tell," there are many things I cannot tell.

God has allowed me to know not only about heaven but also about deep secrets of the spiritual realm for a couple of reasons. First, God wants to save numerous people through my testifying of God who has been since before time began, and by spreading Jesus Christ the Savior. Second, by spreading the holiness gospel, God who is holy and perfect wants to lead His children to become holy and perfect, as beautiful brides prepared for the Lord's return.

Therefore, you should realize that the end is very near. Work toward being able to enter New Jerusalem, which is clear and beautiful as crystal, by spreading the gospel and trying to prepare yourself as a beautiful bride of Christ Jesus.

SECRETS OF HEAVEN REVEALED AT THE END OF TIME

Let us delve into the secrets of heaven that are revealed and are to come to fruition at the end of the time through the parables of Jesus in Matthew 13.

He will separate the wicked from the righteous

Jesus says the kingdom of heaven is like a net that was let down into the lake and caught all kinds of fish. What does this mean?

> Once again, the kingdom of heaven is like a net that was let down into the lake and caught all kinds of fish. When it was full, the fishermen pulled it up on the shore. Then they sat down and collected the good fish in baskets, but threw the bad away. This is how it will be at the end of the age. The angels will come and separate the wicked from the righteous and throw them into the fiery furnace, where there will be weeping and gnashing of teeth.
>
> —MATTHEW 13:47–50

The "lake" here refers to the world, the "fish" to all believers, and the "fisherman" who lets down a net into the lake and catches fish, God. What, then, does it mean for God to let down a net, pull it up when it is full, and collect the good fish in baskets and throw the bad away? This is to let you know that at the end of the time, the angels will come and collect the righteous ones to heaven and throw the bad into hell.

Today, many people think that they will definitely enter the kingdom of heaven if they accept Jesus Christ. Jesus, however, clearly says, "The angels will separate the wicked from the righteous and throw them into the fiery furnace" (v. 49). The "righteous" here implies those who are called "righteous" based on their belief in Jesus Christ in their hearts and the reflection of this belief in their actions. You are "righteous" not because you know God's Word, but only because you obey His commandments and act according to His will (Matt. 7:21).

In the Bible, there are "do's," "don'ts," "keeps," and "throw aways." Only those who live according to the Word of God are righteous and considered to have spiritual, living faith. There are people who are said to be generally righteous, but they can be categorized as "righteous" in the sight of people or "righteous" in the sight of God. Therefore, you should be able to recognize the difference between the righteousness of men and that of God, and become a righteous man in the sight of God.

For instance, if a man who considers himself righteous steals, who will accept him as being righteous? If those who call themselves "children of God," keep committing sins and do not live according to God's Word, they cannot be called "righteous." These kind of people are the wicked among the "righteous."

Each different splendor of the heavenly bodies

If you accept Jesus Christ and live according to only God's

Word, you will be shining like the sun in heaven. The apostle Paul writes on secrets of heaven in detail in 1 Corinthians 15:40–41:

> There are also heavenly bodies and there are earthly bodies; but the splendor of the heavenly bodies is one kind, and the splendor of the earthly bodies is another. The sun has one kind of splendor, the moon another and the stars another; and star differs from star in splendor.

Since one possesses heaven only by faith, it is sensible that the splendor of heaven will be different according to the measure of one's faith. That is why there is a splendor of the sun, of the moon, and of the stars; even among the stars, their measure of brightness differs.

Let us look at another secret of heaven through the parable of a mustard seed in Matthew 13:31–32:

> He told them another parable: "The kingdom of heaven is like a mustard seed, which a man took and planted in his field. Though it is the smallest of all your seeds, yet when it grows, it is the largest of garden plants and becomes a tree, so that the birds of the air come and perch in its branches."

One mustard seed is as small as a dot left by a ballpoint pen. Even this small seed will grow to be a big tree so that the birds of the air come and perch. Then, what did Jesus want to teach us through this parable of the mustard seed? The lessons to be learned are that heaven is possessed by faith, and that there are different measures of faith. So even if you have a "small" faith now, you can nurture it into to a "great" faith.

Even faith as small as a mustard seed

Jesus says, in Matthew 17:20, "Because you have so little

faith. I tell you the truth, if you have faith as small as a mustard seed, you can say to this mountain, 'Move from here to there' and it will move. Nothing will be impossible for you." In response to the demand of His disciples, "Increase our faith!" Jesus replies, "If you have faith as small as a mustard seed, you can say to this mulberry tree, 'Be uprooted and planted in the sea,' and it will obey you" (Luke 17:5–6).

What, then, is the spiritual meaning of these verses? It means that when faith as small as a mustard seed grows and becomes a great faith, nothing will be impossible. When one accepts Jesus Christ, faith as small as a mustard seed is given to him. When he sows this seed in his heart, it will sprout. When it grows into a great faith the size of a big tree where many birds come and perch, one will experience the works of God's power that Jesus performed, such as the blind coming to see, the deaf coming to hear, the mute coming to speak, and the dead coming back to life.

If you think you have faith but cannot show works of God's power and have problems in your family or businesses yet, it is because your faith as small as a mustard seed has not yet grown into the size of a big tree.

The process of the growth of spiritual faith

In 1 John 2:12–14 (NASB), the apostle John briefly explains the growth of spiritual faith:

> I am writing to you, little children, because your sins have been forgiven you for His name's sake. I am writing to you, fathers, because you know Him who has been from the beginning. I am writing to you, young men, because you have overcome the evil one. I have written to you, children, because you know the Father. I have written to you, fathers, because you know Him who has been from the beginning. I have written to you, young men, because you are strong, and the word of God abides in you, and you have overcome the evil one.

You should realize that there is a process in the growth of faith. You must develop your faith and have the faith of fathers, in which you are able to know God who has been since before the beginning of time. You should not be satisfied with the level of children's faith whose sins are forgiven on account of Jesus Christ.

Also, as Jesus says in Matthew 13:33, "The kingdom of heaven is like yeast that a woman took and mixed into a large amount of flour until it worked all through the dough."

Therefore, you ought to understand that growing faith as small as a mustard seed to great faith can be accomplished as quickly as yeast that works all through the dough. As it says in 1 Corinthians 12:9, faith is a spiritual gift given to you by God.

Heaven to buy with all you have

You need actual efforts to possess heaven because heaven can only be possessed by faith, and there is a process in the growth of faith. Even in this world you have to try so hard to gain wealth and fame, not to talk about enough money to buy, for instance, a house. You try so hard to buy and maintain all these things, none of which you can keep forever. How much more, then, would you have to try to get the splendor and dwelling place of heaven that you will have forever?

Jesus says in Matthew 13:44, "The kingdom of heaven is like treasure hidden in a field. When a man found it, he hid it again, and then in his joy went and sold all he had and bought that field." He continues in Matthew 13:45–46, "Again, the kingdom of heaven is like a merchant looking for fine pearls. When he found one of great value, he went away and sold everything he had and bought it."

So, what are the secrets of heaven revealed through the parables of the treasure hidden in a field and of the good pearl? Jesus usually told parables with objects that could easily be found in everyday life. Now let us look at the parable of "the treasure hidden in a field."

There was a poor farmer who made a living by earning daily wages. One day he went to work at the request of his neighbor. The farmer was told that the land was barren because it had not been used for a long time, but his neighbor wanted to plant some fruit trees so as not to waste the land. The farmer agreed to do the work. As he was clearing the land he felt something very solid at the end of the shovel. He continued digging and found so much treasure in the ground. The farmer who discovered the treasure began to think of ways by which he could possess the treasure. He decided to buy the land in which the treasure had been hidden. Since the field was barren and was almost wasted, the farmer thought the owner of the land might want to sell it without much hassle.

The farmer came back to his house, cleared all he had owned, and began to sell his possessions. Yet, he had no regrets to sell everything he had, because he had discovered the treasure, which was worth more than all he had.

The parable of the treasure hidden in a field

What do you have to realize through the parable of the treasure hidden in a field? I hope that you will understand the secret of heaven by looking at the spiritual meaning of the parable of the treasure hidden in a field in four aspects:

First, the field stands for your heart and the treasure stands for heaven. It implies that heaven, like the treasure, is hidden in your heart.

God made human beings with spirit, soul, and body. The spirit is made as the master of a man, and is able to communicate with God. The soul is made to obey the command of the spirit, and the body is made as the dwelling place for the spirit and the soul. Therefore, a human being used to be a living spirit as it says in Genesis 2:7.

Since the time the first man Adam committed the sin of disobedience, however, the spirit, the master of man, died, and the soul began to play the role of the master. People then fell into more sin and had to go to the way of death, because they could no longer communicate with God. They were now people of the soul, which is under the control of the enemy Satan.

For this, God of love sent His one and only Son Jesus to this world and let Him be crucified and shed His blood as the atoning sacrifice to redeem all mankind from their sins. Because of this, the way of salvation has opened for you to become a child of the holy God and communicate with Him again.

Therefore, whoever accepts Jesus Christ as his personal Savior will receive the Holy Spirit, and his spirit will revive. Also, he will receive the right to become God's child and joy will fill his heart.

It means that the spirit came to communicate with God and control the soul and the body again as the master of the human being. This also means that he came to fear God, obey His Word, and carry out the assigned duty of man.

Therefore, revival of the spirit is the same as discovering the treasure hidden in a field. Heaven is like the treasure hidden in a field because heaven is now present in your heart.

Second, a man finding the treasure hidden in a field and being joyful implies that if one accepts Jesus Christ and receives the Holy Spirit, the dead spirit will revive, and he will realize that there is heaven in his heart and rejoice.

Jesus says in Matthew 11:12, "The kingdom of heaven has been forcefully advancing, and forceful men lay hold of it." The apostle John also writes in Revelation 22:14: "Blessed are those who wash their robes, that they may have the right to the tree of life and may go through the gates into the city."

What you can learn through this is that not everybody who has accepted Jesus Christ will go to the same dwelling place in the kingdom of heaven. To the extent that you resemble the Lord and become truthful, you will inherit a more beautiful dwelling place within heaven. Therefore, those who love God and hope for heaven will act according to God's Word in everything and resemble the Lord by casting away all their evilness.

You possess the kingdom of heaven as much as you fill your heart with heaven, where there is only goodness and truth. Even on this earth, when you realize that there is heaven in your heart, you will be joyful. This is the kind of joy you experience when you first meet Jesus Christ. If one who had to go to the way of death instead gained a true life and the eternal heaven through Jesus Christ, how joyful he would be! He would also be so grateful because he could believe in the kingdom of heaven in his heart. In this way, the joy of a man who rejoices for having found out the treasure hidden in a field stands for the joy of accepting Jesus Christ and having the kingdom of heaven in his heart.

Third, hiding the treasure again after finding it implies that one's dead spirit has revived and he wants to live according to God's will, but he cannot really put his determination into action because he has not received the power to live according to God's Word.

The farmer could not immediately dig up the treasure as soon as he found it. He first had to sell his possessions and buy the field. In the same way, you know there are heaven and hell and how you can enter heaven when you accept Jesus Christ, but you cannot show your action as soon as you start listening to the Word of God.

Because you lived an unrighteous life that was in defiance of God's Word before you accepted Jesus Christ, there remains much unrighteousness in your heart. Yet, if you do not cast away all that is untruthful in your heart while professing your belief in God, Satan will continue to lead you to darkness so that you cannot live according to God's Word. Just as the farmer bought the field after selling all he had, you can get the treasure in your heart only when you try to cast away the mind of untruthfulness and have the truthful heart that God wants.

Thus, you have to follow the truth, which is the Word of God, by depending on God and praying fervently. Only then will the untruth be thrown away and you receive the power to act and live according to God's Word. You should keep in mind that heaven is only for this kind of people.

Fourth, selling all he had implies that in order for the dead spirit to revive and become the master of the man again, he has to demolish all untruths belonging to his soul.

When the dead spirit revives, you will realize that there is heaven. You should possess heaven by demolishing all thoughts of untruth, which belong to the soul and are ruled by Satan, and by having the faith accompanied with action. This is the same principle as a chicken having to break the shell to come out into the world.

Therefore, you must cast away all the deeds and desires of the flesh to fully possess heaven. Moreover, you should become a person of the whole spirit who resembles the divine nature of the Lord completely. (See 1 Thessalonians 5:23.)

Deeds of the flesh are the embodiment of evilness in the heart that results in deed. Desires of the flesh refer to all natures of sin in the heart that can result in deed anytime, even though it has not yet resulted in deed. For example, if you have hatred in your heart, it is the desire of the flesh, and if this hatred results in the deed of hitting another person, this is a deed of the flesh.

Galatians 5:19–21 (NASB) firmly states:

> Now the deeds of the flesh are evident, which are: immorality, impurity, sensuality, idolatry, sorcery, enmities, strife, jealousy, outbursts of anger, disputes, dissensions, factions, envying, drunkenness, carousing, and things like these, of which I forewarn you, just as I have forewarned you, that those who practice such things will not inherit the kingdom of God.

Also, Romans 13:13–14 (NASB) tells us, "Let us behave properly as in the day, not in carousing and drunkenness, not in sexual promiscuity and sensuality, not in strife and jealousy. But put on the Lord Jesus Christ, and make no provision for the flesh in regard to its lusts." Romans 8:5 (NASB) says, "For those who are according to the flesh set their minds on the things of the flesh, but those who are according to the Spirit, the things of the Spirit."

Therefore, selling all you have means demolishing all untruth against God's will in your soul and casting away your deeds and desires of the flesh, which are not right according to God's Word, and all the rest that you have loved more than you have loved God.

If you keep on casting away your sins and evilness this way, your spirit revives more and more and you can live according to God's Word following the desire of the Holy Spirit. Finally, you will become a person of spirit and be able to attain the divine nature of the Lord (Phil. 2:5–8).

Heaven possessed as much as accomplished in heart

One who possesses heaven by faith is the one who sells all he has by casting away all evil and accomplishing heaven in his heart. Eventually when the Lord returns, the heaven that has been like a shadow becomes a reality and he will have the eternal heaven. One who possesses heaven is the richest person even if he has thrown everything away in this world. However, one who does not possess heaven is the poorest person who has nothing in reality, even if he has everything in this world. Everything you need is in Jesus Christ and everything outside Jesus Christ is worthless. This is because after death, only the eternal judgment awaits.

That is why Matthew gave up his occupation to follow Jesus. That is why Peter gave up his boat and net to follow Jesus. Even the apostle Paul considered everything he had as rubbish after accepting Jesus Christ. The reason all these apostles could do this was because they wanted to find the treasure, which was worth more than anything in this world, and dig it up.

In the same way, you must show your faith with action by obeying the true Word and casting away all untruths that are against God. You have to accomplish the kingdom of heaven in your heart by selling all untruths such as stubbornness, pride, and haughtiness that you have so far considered as a treasure in your heart. Therefore, you should not look for the things in this world, but sell all you have to accomplish heaven in your heart and inherit the eternal kingdom of heaven.

IN MY FATHER'S HOUSE ARE MANY DWELLING PLACES

From John 14:1–3, you can see that there are many dwelling places in heaven, and Jesus Christ went to prepare a place for you in heaven:

> Do not let your hearts be troubled. Trust in God; trust also in me. In my Father's house are many rooms; if it were not so, I would have told you. I am going there to prepare a place for you. And if I go and prepare a place for you, I will come back and take you to be with me that you also may be where I am.

The Lord went to prepare your heavenly place

Jesus told His disciples the things that would take place just before He was captured for the crucifixion. Looking at His disciples, who were worried after hearing about the betrayal of Judas Iscariot, the denial of Peter, and the death of Jesus, He comforted them by telling them about the dwelling places of heaven.

That is why He said, "In my Father's house are many rooms; if it were not so, I would have told you. I am going there to prepare a place for you." Jesus was crucified and really resurrected after three days, breaking the authority of death. Then, after forty days He ascended into heaven while many people watched, to prepare heavenly places for you.

Then, what does it mean by: "I am going there to prepare a place for you"? As written in 1 John 2:2, "He is the atoning sacrifice for our sins, and not only for ours but also for the sins of the whole world," it means that Jesus broke the wall of sins between men and God, so anybody can possess heaven by faith.

Without Jesus Christ, the wall of sins between God and you could not have been toppled. In the Old Testament, when a man committed sins he offered an animal sacrifice to atone for his sin. Jesus, however, enabled you to be forgiven of your sins and to become holy by offering Himself as a one-time sacrifice. (See Hebrews 10:12–14.) Only through Jesus Christ can the wall of sin between God and you be toppled. Only through Him can you receive the blessing of entering the kingdom of heaven and enjoying the beautiful and happy eternal life.

In my Father's house are many dwelling places

Jesus in John 14:2 says, "In my Father's house are many dwelling places." The heart of the Lord who wants everybody to be saved is melted in this verse. By the way, what is the reason why Jesus said "In my Father's house," instead of saying, "In the kingdom of heaven"? It is because God does not want "citizens" but "children" with whom He can share His love forever as a Father.

Heaven is ruled by God and is big enough to accomodate all those who are saved by faith. Also, it is such a beautiful and fantastic place that cannot be compared to this world. In the kingdom of heaven, whose size is unimaginable, the most beautiful and glorious place is New Jerusalem where God's throne is. Just as there is the Blue House in Seoul, the capital of Korea, and the White House in Washington, DC, the capital of the United States, for the president of each country to live in, in New Jerusalem is the throne of God.

Then, where is New Jerusalem? It is in the center of heaven, and it is the place where the people of faith who pleased God will live forever. Conversely, the most outer part of heaven is Paradise. Like the one robber on one side of Jesus who accepted Jesus Christ and was saved, those who only accepted Jesus Christ and did not do anything for the kingdom of God will stay there.

Heaven is given according to the measure of faith

Why has God prepared many dwelling places in heaven for His children? God is righteous and makes you reap what you sow (Gal. 6:7), and rewards each person according to what he has done (Matt. 16:27; Rev. 2:23). That is why He prepared the dwelling places according to the measure of faith.

Romans 12:3 observes, "For by the grace given me I say to every one of you: Do not think of yourself more highly than you ought, but rather think of yourself with sober judgment, in accordance with the measure of faith God has given you." Therefore, you should realize that the dwelling place and the glory of each person in heaven would differ according to his measure of faith.

Depending on the extent to which you resemble the heart of God, your dwelling place in heaven will be determined. The dwelling place in the eternal heaven will be decided according to how much you have accomplished heaven in your heart as a spiritual person.

For example, let us say a child and an adult are competing in a sporting event or having a discussion. The world of children and that of adults are so different that children would soon find it boring to be with adults. For children, their way of thinking, language, and actions are so different from those of the adults. It would be fun when children play with children, youths with youths, and adults with adults.

This is the same spiritually. Since everybody's spirit is different, the God of love and righteousness has divided the dwelling places of heaven according to the measure of faith so that His children will live happily.

The Lord comes after preparing heavenly dwelling places

In John 14:3, the Lord promised that He would come back and take you to the kingdom of heaven after He finishes preparing the dwelling places in heaven.

Suppose there is a man who once received God's grace and had many rewards in heaven because he was faithful. But if he goes back to the ways of the world, he falls from salvation and ends up in hell. And his many heavenly rewards will become worthless. Even if he does not go to hell, his rewards may still become nothing.

Sometimes if he disappoints God by disgracing Him though he was once faithful, or if he goes back a level or stays at the same level in his Christian life although he should only make progress, his rewards will diminish.

Yet, the Lord will remember everything you have worked and tried for the kingdom of God being faithful. Also, if you sanctify your heart by circumcising it in the Holy Spirit, you will be with the Lord when He comes back and you will be blessed to stay in a place shining like the sun in heaven. Because the Lord wants all children of God to be perfect, He said, "I will come back and take you to be with me that you also may be where I am." Jesus wants you to clean yourself just as the Lord is clean, holding fast to this word of hope.

When Jesus accomplished God's will completely and glorified Him greatly, God glorified Jesus and gave Him a new name: "King of kings, Lord of lords." In the same way, as much as you glorify God in this world, God will lead you to glory. To the extent to which you resemble God and are loved by God, you will live closer to the throne of God in heaven.

Dwelling places of heaven are waiting for their masters, the children of God, just like brides who are prepared to receive their bridegrooms. That is why the apostle John writes in Revelation 21:2: "I saw the Holy City, the new Jerusalem, coming down out of heaven from God, prepared as a bride beautifully dressed for her husband."

Even the best services of a beautiful bride of this world cannot be compared to the comfort and happiness of the dwelling places of heaven. Houses in heaven have everything and provide everything by reading the mind of the masters so that they would live most happily forever.

Proverbs 17:3 notes: "The crucible for silver and the furnace for gold, but the LORD tests the heart." Therefore, I pray in the name of the Lord that you realize that God refines people to make them His true children, sanctify yourself with the hope for New Jerusalem, and forcefully advance toward the best of heaven by being faithful in God's house.

CHAPTER 5
HOW WILL WE LIVE IN HEAVEN?

> There are also heavenly bodies and there are earthly bodies; but the splendor of the heavenly bodies is one kind, and the splendor of the earthly bodies is another. The sun has one kind of splendor, the moon another and the stars another; and star differs from star in splendor.
>
> —1 CORINTHIANS 15:40–41

The happiness in heaven cannot be compared even to the best and most delightful things on this earth. Even if you enjoy yourself with your loved ones on a beach with the horizon in sight, this kind of happiness is only momentary and not true. In one corner of your mind there are still worries about the things to face after returning to your everyday life. If you repeat this kind of life for a month or two, or for a year, you will soon get bored and begin to look for something new.

However, the life in heaven, where everything is as clear and beautiful as crystal, is the happiness itself because everything is new, mysterious, joyful, and happy continually. You can have delightful times with God the Father and the Lord, or you can enjoy your hobbies, favorite games, and all other interesting things as much as you want. Let us look into how the children of God will live when they go to heaven.

AN OVERALL LIFESTYLE IN HEAVEN

As your physical body will change into a spiritual body, which consists of the spirit, the soul, and the body in heaven, you will be able to recognize your wife, husband, children, and parents on this earth. You will also recognize your shepherd or your flock on this earth. And you will also remember what has been forgotten on this earth. You will be very wise because you will be able to distinguish and understand God's will.

Some may wonder, "Will all my sins be exposed in heaven?" This will not be so. If you have already repented, God will not remember your sins as far as the east is from the west (Ps. 103:12), but only remember your good deeds because all your sins will have already been forgiven by the time you are in heaven.

Then, when you go to heaven, how will you change and live?

The heavenly body

Human beings and animals on this earth have their own shapes so that every living thing is recognizable, whether it is an elephant, a lion, an eagle, or a human being.

Just as there is a body with its own shape in this three-dimensional world, there is a unique body in heaven, which is a four-dimensional world. This is called the heavenly body. In heaven you will recognize each other by this. Then, what will a heavenly body look like?

When the Lord returns in the air, each of you changes into the resurrected body that is the spiritual body. This resurrected body will transform into the heavenly body, which is in a higher level, after the Great Judgment. According to each one's rewards, the light of glory that shines from this heavenly body will be different.

A heavenly body has bones and flesh like the body of Jesus right after His resurrection (see John 20:27), but it is the new body that consists of a spirit, a soul, and an imperishable body. Our perishable body is changing into a new body by the Word and power of God.

The heavenly body consisting of eternally imperishable bones and flesh will shine because it is refreshed and clean.

Even if one is missing an arm or a leg, or handicapped, the heavenly body will be recovered as the perfect body.

The heavenly body is not faint like a shadow but has a clear shape, and is not under the control of time and space. That is why when Jesus appeared before the disciples after His resurrection, He could go through the walls freely. (See John 20:26.)

The body on this earth will have wrinkles and be rough when it gets old, but the heavenly body will be refreshed as an imperishable body so that it will always keep its youth and shine like the sun.

Age of thirty-three

Many people wonder whether the heavenly body is as big as that of an adult or as small as that of a child. In heaven, everybody, whether or not one died young or old, will eternally have the youth of the age thirty-three, the age of Jesus when He was crucified on this earth.

Why does God let you live at the age of thirty-three forever in heaven? Just as the sun is the brightest at noon, around the age of thirty-three is the peak time in one's life.

Those who are younger than thirty may be a little inexperienced and immature, and those who are above forty lose their energy as they get old. Yet, around the age of thirty-three, people are mature and beautiful in all aspects. Also, most of them get married, give birth, and raise children so that they understand, to some extent, the heart of God who cultivates human beings on this earth.

In this way, God changes you into a heavenly body so that you will keep the youth of the age of thirty-three, the most beautiful age of human beings, forever in heaven.

There is no biological relationship

If you live in heaven forever with the physical appearance of the time you leave this world, how funny would that be?

Heaven I

Let us say that a man died at the age of forty and went to heaven. His son went to heaven at the age of fifty, and his grandson died at the age of ninety and went to heaven. When they all meet together in heaven, the grandson would be the oldest, and the grandfather would be the youngest.

Therefore, in heaven where God rules with His righteousness and love, everybody will be thirty-three years old, and the biological or physical relationship of this earth does not apply.

No one calls anyone else 'father', 'mother', 'son', or 'daughter' in heaven although they were parents and children on this earth. It is because everybody is a brother and sister to each other as a child of God. Since they know they had been parents and children on this earth and loved each other very much, they can have more special love for each other.

What if, however, the mother went to the Second Kingdom of heaven and her son to New Jerusalem? On this earth, of course, the son has to serve the mother. In heaven, however, the mother will bow to her son because he resembles God the Father more, and the light that comes out from his heavenly body will be much brighter than her own.

Therefore, you do not call others by the names and titles you use on this earth, but God the Father gives the new, appropriate names that have spiritual meanings to each one. Even on this earth, God changed the name Abram to Abraham, Sarai to Sarah, and Jacob to Israel (which means that Jacob had struggled with God and had overcome).

Difference between men and women in heaven

In heaven there is no marriage, but there still is a clear distinction between men and women. First of all, men have the height of six feet to six-feet, two-inches and the women are about four inches shorter.

Some people worry so much about their height being too short or too tall, but there is no need of such concern in heaven. Also, there is no need to worry about one's weight because everybody will have the most suitable and beautiful shape.

A heavenly body does not feel any weight even though it seems to have weight, so that even if one walks on flowers they do not get pressed or crumbled. A heavenly body cannot be weighed, but is not something to be blown by winds because it is very stable. Having weight even though you cannot feel it means that you have a shape and an appearance. It is like when you lift up a sheet of paper, you do not feel any weight but you know it does have some weight.

Men's hair comes down to the neck, but the length of women's hair differs from one another. Having long hair for a woman means that she has received great rewards, and the longest hair comes down to the waist. Therefore, it is a tremendous glory and pride to have long hair for women. (See 1 Corinthians 11:15.)

On this earth, most women hope and try to have soft skin. They apply cosmetic products to keep their skin tight and soft without any wrinkles. In heaven, everybody will have spotless skin that is so clear, and clean, shining with the light of glory.

Moreover, since there is no evil in heaven, there is no need to wear makeup or worry about outward appearances because everything looks beautiful there. The light of glory that comes out from the heavenly body will shine whiter, clearer, and brighter according to the extent that each one became fully sanctified and resembled the heart of the Lord. Also, the order is decided and maintained by this.

The heart of heavenly people

The people with the heavenly body have the heart of the spirit itself, which is in the divine nature and has no evil at all. Just as people want to have and touch what is good and beautiful on this earth, even the hearts of people with the heavenly bodies want to feel the beauty of others, look at them, and touch them with delight. Yet, there is no greed or envy at all.

Also, people change according to their own benefit on this earth, and they feel tired of things, even if they are pretty and good things. The hearts of people with the heavenly bodies have no slyness and never change. For example, poor people on this earth can eat cheap, low-quality food and find it delicious. If they become a little richer, they are not satisfied with what used to be delicious and begin looking for better food. If you buy a new toy for a child, they are very happy in the beginning, but after several days they will feel repugnant toward it and look for a new one. In heaven, however, there is no such mind-set. If you like anything once, you will like it forever.

CLOTHING IN HEAVEN

Some may think that the clothing in heaven will be the same, but that is not the case. God is the Creator and the Righteous Judge who gives back according to what you have done. Therefore, just as rewards in heaven are different, the clothes will also be different according to the deeds on this earth (Rev. 22:12). Then, what kind of clothes would you have on and how do you decorate them in heaven?

Heavenly clothes with different color and design

In heaven, everybody basically wears bright, white, and shiny clothes. They are soft as silk and so light as though they had no weight, and swing beautifully.

Because the extent to which each one is sanctified is different, the lights that come out from the clothes and the brightness are different. The more one resembles God's holy heart, the more brightly and brilliantly his clothes will shine. Also, depending on the amount you worked for the kingdom of God and glorified Him, various kinds of clothes with many different designs and materials will be given accordingly.

On this earth, people wear different kinds of clothes according to their social and economic status. Likewise, in heaven you will wear clothes with more colors and designs as you get into a higher position in heaven. Also, hairstyles and accessories are different.

Moreover, in old days people recognized each other's social class just by looking at the colors of their clothes. In the same way, heavenly people can recognize the position and the volume of rewards given to each one in heaven. Wearing clothes of specified colors and designs different from others means that one has received the greater glory. Therefore, those who have entered New Jerusalem or contributed much for the kingdom of God receive the most beautiful, colorful, and brilliant clothes.

Heavenly clothes with different decorations

God will give clothes with different decorations to show the glory of each one. Just as a royal family of the past expressed their positions by placing special decorations on their clothes, the clothes in heaven with different decorations will show one's heavenly position and glory.

There are decorations of thanks, praise, prayer, joy, glory, and so forth that can be sewn into the clothes in heaven. When you sing praises in this life with a thankful mind for the love and grace of God the Father and the Lord, or when you sing to glorify God, He receives your heart as a beautiful aroma and He puts the decoration of praise on your clothes in heaven.

The decorations of joy and thanks will be placed beautifully for the people who have been truly joyful and thankful in their hearts by remembering the grace of God the Father who gave eternal life and the kingdom of heaven even during sorrows and trials on earth.

Next, the decoration of prayer will be for those who have prayed with their life for the kingdom of God. Among all these, however, the most beautiful decoration is the decoration of glory. This is the most difficult to earn. This is only given to those who did everything for the glory of God from their true hearts. Just as a king or a president rewards a special honorary medal to a soldier who rendered distinguished services, this decoration of glory is particularly given to those who worked arduously for the kingdom of God and gave great glory to Him. Therefore, the one who puts on the clothes with the decoration of glory is one of the most noble of all in the kingdom of heaven.

Rewards of crowns and jewels

There are countless jewels in heaven. And some jewels are given as rewards and are put on clothes. In the Book of Revelation you read that the Lord is wearing a golden crown and a sash around His chest, and these are also rewards given to Him by God.

The Bible mentions many kinds of crowns. The standards by which to receive crowns and the values of crowns are different because they are given as rewards.

There are many kinds of crowns given according to each one's deeds, such as an imperishable crown given to those who compete in games (1 Cor. 9:25), the crown of glory given to those who glorified God (1 Pet. 5:4), the crown of life given to those who were faithful to the point of death (James 1:12; Rev. 2:10), the golden crown that the twenty-four elders are wearing around the throne of God (Rev. 4:4; 14:14), and the crown of righteousness for which the apostle Paul longed (2 Tim. 4:8).

Also, there are crowns of many shapes that are decorated with jewels, such as the gold-decorated crown, the crown of flowers, the crown of pearls, and so on. By the kind of crown one receives, you can recognize his holiness and rewards.

On this earth, if a person has money they can buy jewels, but in heaven you can have jewels only when they are given to you as rewards. Factors such as the number of people you led to salvation, the amount of the offering you rendered with true heart, and the extent of your faithfulness determine various kinds of rewards to be given. Therefore, the jewels and crowns must be different because they are given according to each one's deeds. Also, the light, beauty, splendor, and the number of jewels and crowns are different as well.

It is the same with the dwelling places and houses of heaven. The dwelling places differ according to each one's faith; the size, beauty, brightness of gold, and other jewels for the personal houses are all different. From chapter six onward, we will take a closer look at the details about the dwelling places of heaven.

FOOD IN HEAVEN

When the first man Adam and Eve lived in the Garden of Eden, they ate only fruits and seed-bearing plants (Genesis 1:29). However, when they were driven out from the Garden of Eden because of their disobedience, they came to eat the plants of the field. After the great flood, people were allowed to eat meat. In this way, as man became more evil, the kind of food changed accordingly.

What, then, will you eat in heaven, where there is no evil at all? Some might wonder if the heavenly body also has to eat. In heaven, you can drink the water of life and eat or smell many kinds of fruits to receive joy.

Heavenly smells

To "smell" here refers to the breathing of the spirit. Of course, the heavenly body does not have to breathe at all, but it can rest while breathing the way you breathe on this earth. So it can breathe not only with the nose and mouth, but also with the eyes and all the cells of the body, even with the heart.

God also uses His sense of smell because He is spirit. That

is why God was pleased with the sacrifices of righteous men and smelled the aroma in the Old Testament (Gen. 8:21). In the New Testament, Jesus, who is pure and spotless, became a sacrifice Himself with a beautiful aroma (Eph. 5:2).

Therefore, God receives the aroma of your heart when you worship, pray, or sing praises with a true heart. As much as you resemble the Lord and become righteous, you become the aroma of the Christ, and in turn are received as a precious offering to God. God receives your praises and prayers with pleasure through smelling.

In Matthew 26:29 you see that the Lord has been praying for you ever since He ascended into heaven, without eating anything for the last two millennia. Likewise, in heaven the heavenly body can live even without eating or smelling. You yourself will live forever when you go to heaven because you will change into a spiritual body that never perishes.

When the heavenly body uses its sense of smell, however, it can feel more joy and happiness and the spirit becomes rejuvenated and renewed. Just as people balance their diets to maintain their health, the heavenly body enjoys smelling in heaven.

So when many kinds of flowers and fruits give out their aroma, the heavenly body smells through breathing. Even if it smells the same aroma time and again, it will feel the same happiness and satisfaction.

Moreover, when a heavenly body smells the beautiful aroma of flowers and fruits, the aroma soaks into the body like perfume. The body gives out the aroma until it completely disappears. As you feel good when you put on perfume on this earth, the heavenly body feels happier to smell because of the beautiful aroma.

Discharge through the breath

How, then, do people eat and continue their lives in heaven? In the Bible you see that the Lord appeared before

His disciples after His resurrection, and either breathed out (John 20:22) or had some food (John 21:12–15). The reason the resurrected Lord had some food was not because He was hungry. He ate to share the joy with the disciples and let you know that you too will eat in heaven as a heavenly body. That is why the Bible recorded that Christ Jesus had some bread and fish for breakfast after His resurrection.

Then, why does the Bible tell you that the Lord breathed out even after He resurrected? When you have food in heaven, it dissolves immediately and gets discharged through the breath. In heaven, when food is eaten it disintegrates in an instant and leaves the body through the breath. So there is no need for excretion or toilets. How comfortable and wondrous it is that the food consumed is dissolved and leaves the body through the breath as aroma!

TRANSPORTATION IN HEAVEN

Throughout the history of mankind, as civilizations and science advanced, faster and more comfortable means of transportation such as carts, wagons, automobiles, ships, trains, airplanes, and so on have been invented.

There are many kinds of transportation in heaven as well. There is a public transportation system, like the train of heaven, and there are private means of transportation such as cloud automobiles and golden wagons.

In heaven the heavenly body can go very fast or even fly because it goes beyond space and time, but it is more fun and delightful to use the transportation given as rewards.

Travel and transportation in heaven

How happy and joyful it would be if you could travel all around heaven and see all the beautiful and wondrous things that God has made!

Every corner of heaven has a unique beauty so you can enjoy every part of it. Yet, because the heart of the heavenly body never changes, it never gets bored or tired of visiting the same place again. So traveling in heaven is always such a fun and interesting thing to do.

The heavenly body does not really have to be on any kind of transportation because it never gets exhausted and can even fly. However, the use of various vehicles makes it feel all the more comfortable. It is similar to how riding on a bus is a little more comfortable than walking and riding in a taxi or driving a car is a little more comfortable than riding on a bus or taking the subway.

So if you ride on the train of heaven, which is decorated with many colorful jewels, you can go to your destination even without any railway. The train can move freely to the right and the left, or even up and down.

When the people in Paradise go to the New Jerusalem, they will ride on the train of heaven because the two places are quite distant from each other. This is a great thrill for the passengers. Flying through bright lights, they can see the beautiful scenery of heaven through the windows. They feel even happier at the thought of seeing God the Father.

Among the transportation in heaven, there is the golden wagon that a special person in the New Jerusalem rides when he goes around heaven. It has white wings, and there is a button inside. With the push of that button the wagon becomes fully automatic and can run or even fly as the owner wishes.

Cloud automobile

The clouds in heaven are like a decoration to add to the beauty of heaven. So when the heavenly body goes to places with the clouds around it, the body shines more than going without the clouds. It can also make others feel and revere the dignity, glory, and authority of the clouded spiritual body.

The Bible says that the Lord is coming with the clouds (1 Thess. 4:16–17), and this is because coming with the clouds of glory is much more majestic, dignified, and beautiful than coming in the air without anything. In the same way, clouds in heaven exist to add glory to the children of God.

If you are qualified to enter the New Jerusalem, you can possess the more wondrous cloud automobile. It is not a cloud formed by vapor like on this earth, but is made of the cloud of glory in heaven.

The cloud automobile shows the glory, dignity, and authority of its owner. However, not everybody can possess a cloud automobile. It is given only to those who are qualified to enter New Jerusalem by having been completely sanctified and faithful in all God's house.

Those who enter New Jerusalem can go anywhere with the Lord riding on this cloud automobile. During the ride, the heavenly host and angels escort and serve them. It is just like many ministers who serve a king or a prince when he is on the road. Therefore, the escort and service of the heavenly host and angels further show the authority and glory of the owner.

The cloud automobiles are usually driven by angels. There are one-seaters for private use, or multiple-seaters in which many people can ride together. When a person in New Jerusalem plays golf and moves around the field, a cloud automobile comes and stops at the master's feet. When the master gets in the vehicle, it moves to the ball very softly in a moment.

Imagine you are flying in the sky, riding in a cloud automobile with the escort of the heavenly hosts and angels in New Jerusalem. Also, imagine you are riding a cloud automobile with the Lord, or you are traveling the vast great heaven on the train of heaven with your loved ones. You would probably be overwhelmed with joy.

ENTERTAINMENT IN HEAVEN

Some may think that there is not much fun living as a heavenly body, but it is not so. You get tired of or cannot be satisfied fully with the fun in this physical world, but in the spiritual world "fun" always feels new and refreshing.

So even in this world, the more you accomplish the whole spirit, the deeper love you can experience and the happier you are. In heaven, you can enjoy not only your hobbies but also many kinds of entertainment, which are incomparably more enjoyable than any other forms of entertainment on this earth.

Enjoying hobbies and games

Just as people on this earth develop their talents and make their lives more abundant through their hobbies, you can have and enjoy hobbies in heaven as well. You can relish, as much as you want, not only what you liked on this earth, but also the things that you abstained from enjoying in order to do God's works. You can also learn new things.

Those who are interested in musical instruments can praise God playing the harp. Or you can learn to play the piano, flute, and many other instruments. You can also learn them very quickly because everybody becomes much wiser in heaven.

You can also have conversations with nature and heavenly animals to add to your delight. Even plants and animals recognize the children of God, welcome them, and express their love and respect for them.

Furthermore, you can enjoy many sports such as tennis, basketball, bowling, golf, and hang-gliding. However, some sporting events cannot be enjoyed, such as wrestling or boxing, which can harm others. For the sports that are available, the facilities and equipments are not dangerous at all. They are made of wondrous materials and are decorated with gold and jewels to provide you with more happiness and pleasure while enjoying the sport.

Also, the sports equipment recognize the hearts of the people and give more pleasure. For example, if you enjoy bowling, the ball or the pins change their colors and set their positions and distances as you like. The pins fall with beautiful lights and cheerful sound. If you want your partner to win, the pins move according to your desire to make you happier.

In heaven, there is no evil that wants to win or defeat somebody else. Giving more pleasure and benefit to others is winning the game. Some might question the meaning of the game that has neither a winner nor a loser, but in heaven you do not get pleasure by winning against somebody. Playing the game itself is joy.

Of course, there are some games with which you get pleasure through a good and fair competition. For example, there is a game in which you win according to how much fragrance you breathe in from flowers, who has the best way of mixing them to give out the best odor, and the like.

Various types of entertainments

Some of those who like games ask if there is such a thing as an arcade in heaven. Of course there are many games that are much more enjoyable than the ones on this earth.

Games in heaven, unlike the ones on this earth, never tire you or worsen your eyesight. You never feel bored with them. Instead, you feel rejuvenated and at peace after playing them. When you win or get the best score, you feel the most pleasure and you never lose interest.

People in heaven are in heavenly bodies, so they never feel scared of falling from rides such as roller coasters in amusement parks. They only feel the thrill and pleasure. People who suffered from acrophobia on this earth can enjoy those things in heaven as much as they want.

Even if you fall from the roller coaster, you do not get injured because you are a heavenly body. You can land very safely like a master of some martial art, or the angels will protect you. So imagine riding a roller coaster, and screaming with the Lord and all your loved ones. How happy and delightful that would be!

WORSHIP, EDUCATION, AND CULTURE IN HEAVEN

There is no need to work for food, clothing, and housing in heaven. So some may wonder, "What are we going to do forever? Won't we become helpless idling away?" However, there is no need to worry at all.

In heaven, there are so many things you can happily enjoy. There are many kinds of interesting and exciting activities and events like games, education, worship services, parties, festivals, traveling, and sports.

You are not required or forced to partake in these activities. Everybody does everything voluntarily, and does with joy because everything you do gives you an abundant amount of happiness.

Worship with joy before God the Creator

Just as you attend services and worship God at a specific time on this earth, you worship God at certain times in heaven, too. Of course, God preaches the message and through His messages you can learn about God's origin and the spiritual realm that has neither a beginning nor an end.

Generally, those who excel in their studies look forward to the classes and to seeing the Teacher. Even in the life of faith, those who love God and worship in spirit and truth look forward to various worship services and to listening to the voice of the Shepherd who preaches the Word of life.

When you go to heaven, you have joy and happiness in worshiping God and look forward to hearing God's Word. You can listen to God's Word through the services or have times to talk with God. Also, there are times for prayer. Yet, you do not kneel down to pray with your eyes closed as you do on this earth. Prayer is the time to chat with God. Prayers in heaven are conversations with God the Father, the Lord, and the Holy Spirit. How happy and delightful those times would be!

You can also praise God like you do on this earth. Yet, it is not in any language of this world, but you will praise God with new songs. Those who went through trials together or the members of the same church on this earth gather along with their shepherd to worship and to have a time of fellowship.

Then, how do people worship together in heaven, especially since their dwelling places are at different locations throughout heaven? In heaven, the lights of heavenly bodies differ in each dwelling place, so they borrow the appropriate clothes to go to other places of higher level. Therefore, to attend worship services held in New Jerusalem, which is covered with the light of glory, all the people in other places must borrow the appropriate clothes.

By the way, just as you can attend and watch the same service through satellite all over the world at the same time, you can do the same thing in heaven. You can attend and watch the service held in New Jerusalem from all other places of heaven, but the screen in heaven is so natural that you will feel as if you were attending the service in person.

Also, you can invite forefathers of faith like Moses and the apostle Paul and worship together. However, you must have an appropriate spiritual authority to invite those noble figures.

Learning about new and deep spiritual secrets

The children of God learn many spiritual things while they are being cultivated on this earth, but what they learn here is only a step to take to go to heaven. After entering heaven, they begin to learn about the new world.

For example, when believers of Jesus Christ die, except for those who are going to New Jerusalem, they stay in the area located at the edge of Paradise, and there they begin to learn etiquettes and rules of heaven from the angels.

Just as people on this earth must be educated to adapt to their society as they grow, in order to live in the new world of the spiritual realm, you have to be taught in detail how to conduct yourself.

Some may wonder why they still have to study in heaven while they are already learning many things on this earth. Learning on this earth is a spiritual training process, and the real learning begins only after you enter heaven.

Likewise, there is no end to learning because God's kingdom is limitless and lasts forever more. No matter how much you learn, you cannot learn completely about God who has been since before the beginning. You can never fully know the depth of God who has been in presence from everlasting, who has been controlling the whole universe and all things therein, and who will be there to everlasting.

Therefore, you can realize that there are countless things to learn if you go into the limitless spiritual realm, and spiritual learning is very interesting and fun, unlike some studies of this world.

Moreover, spiritual learning is never compulsory and there is no test. You never forget what you learn, so it is never hard or exhausting. You will never be bored or idle in heaven. You will just be happy to learn wondrous and new things.

Parties, banquets, and performances

There are many kinds of parties and performances in heaven as well. These parties are the pinnacles of pleasure in heaven. It is where you enjoy delight and joy from watching the richness, freeness, beauty, and glory of heaven at a glance.

Just as people on this earth decorate themselves most beautifully to go to prestigious parties, and eat, drink, and enjoy the best things, you can have parties with the people who decorate themselves most beautifully. The parties are filled with beautiful dances, songs, and sounds of laughter of happiness.

Also, there are places like Carnegie Hall in New York City or the Sydney Opera House in Australia where you can enjoy various performances. Performances in heaven are not to boast oneself but only to glorify God, give joy and happiness to the Lord, and share with others.

The performers are mostly the ones who glorified God greatly with praises, dances, musical instruments, and plays on this earth. Sometimes these people may perform the same music pieces they performed on this earth. Or, those who wanted to do these things on this earth but could not under their given circumstances can praise God with new songs and new dances in heaven.

Also, there are movie theaters in which you can see movies. In the First or the Second Kingdom, they usually watch movies in public theaters. In the Third Kingdom and New Jerusalem, each resident has his own facility in his house. People can see movies by themselves or invite their loved ones for a movie while having snacks.

In the Bible, the apostle Paul had been to the Third Heaven, but could not reveal it to others (2 Cor. 12:4). It is very hard to make people understand heaven because it is not a world known or understood well by people. Instead, there is a good chance that people will misunderstand. Heaven belongs to the spiritual realm. There are so many things that you cannot understand or imagine in heaven, where it is full of happiness and joy that you can never experience on this earth.

God has prepared such a beautiful heaven for you to live in, and He is encouraging you to have proper qualifications to enter it through the Bible. Therefore, I pray in the name of the Lord that you can receive the Lord with joy with proper qualifications that are necessary to be ready as His beautiful bride when He comes back again.

CHAPTER 6

PARADISE

Jesus answered him, "I tell you the truth, today
you will be with me in paradise."

—LUKE 23:43

All those who believe in Jesus Christ as their personal Savior
and whose names are recorded in the Book of Life will be able
to enjoy eternal life in heaven. I have already explained, however, there are steps in the growth of faith, and the dwelling
places, crowns, and rewards given in heaven will depend on
each one's measure of faith. Those who resemble God's heart
more will live closer to God's throne, and the farther they stay
from God's throne, the less they resemble God's heart.

Paradise is the farthest place from God's throne, has the
least light of God's glory, and is the lowest level in heaven. Yet,
it is still incomparably more beautiful than this earth, even
more beautiful than the Garden of Eden.

Then, what kind of place is Paradise and what kind of people go there?

THE BEAUTY AND HAPPINESS
OF PARADISE

The area on the edge of Paradise is used as the Waiting Place
until the Great Judgment Day of the White Throne (Rev.
20:11–12). Those who went to New Jerusalem after having
accomplished God's heart on earth are helping with God's
works. Everybody else saved from the beginning of time is
waiting in areas on the edge of Paradise.

So you realize Paradise is so wide that its areas around the edge are being used as the Waiting Place for so many people. Although this wide Paradise is the lowest level of heaven, it is still an incomparably more beautiful and happier place than this earth, the place cursed by God. Furthermore, because it is a place where those who are cultivated on this earth will enter, there is so much more happiness and joy than in the Garden of Eden where the first man Adam had lived.

Now, let us look at the beauty and the happiness of Paradise, which God has revealed and made known.

Wide plains full of beautiful animals and plants

Paradise is like a wide plain, and there are many well-organized grass plots and beautiful gardens. Many angels maintain and take care of these places. Singings of the birds are so clear and pure, and they echo throughout the whole Paradise. They look almost like the birds of this earth, but they are a little bigger and have more beautiful feathers. Their singing in groups is so lovely.

Also, trees and flowers in the gardens are so fresh and gorgeous. Trees and flowers of this earth wither with the passage of time, but trees are always green and the flowers never wither in Paradise. When people approach them, flowers smile, and sometimes they give out their unique and blended scents to a distance.

Fresh trees bear many kinds of fruits. They are a little bigger than fruits of this earth. The skins are shiny and they look very delicious. You do not have to peel the skins off because there is no dust or worms. How beautiful and happy would be the scene in which people sit around on a beautiful plain and have conversations, with baskets full of delicious and appetizing fruits?

Also, there are many animals on the wide plain. Among them are lions that feed on the grass peacefully, too. They are much bigger than lions on this earth, but are not aggressive at all. They are so lovely because they have mild characters and clean, shiny hair.

The River of the Water of Life flows quietly

The River of the Water of Life flows throughout heaven, from New Jerusalem to Paradise, and it never vaporizes or becomes polluted. The water from this river originates from the throne of God and refreshes everything that represents the heart of God. It is the clear and beautiful mind that is spotless, blameless and brilliant without any darkness. The heart of God is perfect and complete in everything.

The River of the Water of Life that quietly flows is like twinkling seawater on a sunny day reflecting the sunshine. It is so clear and transparent that it cannot be compared to any body of water on this earth. Looking from some distance, it looks blue and is like the blue deep sea of the Mediterranean or the Atlantic Ocean.

There are beautiful benches on the roads on each side of the River of the Water of Life. Around the benches are trees of life that yield fruit every month. The fruits of the tree of life are bigger than fruits of this earth, and they smell and taste so delicious that they cannot be adequately described. They melt like cotton candy when you put one of them into your mouth.

No personal property in Paradise

In heaven, the hair of men comes down to the neckline, but that of women reflects the amount of rewards given. The longest hair of a woman can come down to the waist. People in Paradise, however, receive no rewards, so women's hair is just a little longer than men's.

They wear white clothing woven in one piece, but there is no decoration like a brooch for clothes or any crowns or pins for hair. It is because they did not do anything for the kingdom of God when they lived on this earth.

Likewise, since all those who go to Paradise have no rewards, there is no personal house, crown, decorations, or angels assigned to serve them. There is just a place for the spirits who live in Paradise to stay. They live in the place serving one another. It is similar to the Garden of Eden in that there is no personal house for each occupant, but there is a significant difference in the magnitude of happiness between the two places. People in Paradise can call God "Abba Father" because they accepted Jesus Christ and received the Holy Spirit, so they feel happiness that cannot be compared with the happiness of the Garden of Eden.

Therefore, it is such a blessing and precious thing that you are born in this world, experience all kinds of good and bad things, become the true children of God, and have faith.

Paradise is full of happiness and joy

Even life in Paradise is full of happiness and joy within the truth because there is no evil and everybody seeks the benefit of others first. Nobody harms anybody but only serves each other with love. How delightful this life would be! Moreover, not having to worry about housing, clothing, and food, and the fact that there are no tears, sorrow, diseases, pain, or death is happiness itself.

> He will wipe every tear from their eyes. There will
> be no more death or mourning or crying or pain,
> for the old order of things has passed away.
> —REVELATION 21:4

You also see that just as there are chief angels among all the angels, there is a hierarchy among the people of Paradise, i.e. representatives and the represented. Because each one's acts of faith are different, those who have relatively greater faith are appointed as representatives to take care of a place or a group of people.

These people wear different clothes than do the ordinary

people of Paradise and have priority in everything. This is not something unjust, but is carried out by God's unbiased justice to give back according to one's deeds. Because there is no jealousy or envy in heaven, people never hate it or get offended when better things are given to others. Instead, they are happy and glad to see others receiving good things. You should realize that Paradise is incomparably the more beautiful and happier place than this earth.

WHAT KIND OF PEOPLE GO TO PARADISE?

Paradise is a beautiful place that is made within God's great love and mercy. It is a place for those who are not qualified enough to be called true children of God but have known God and believed in Jesus Christ, and therefore cannot be sent to hell. Then, exactly what kind of people go to Paradise?

Repenting just before death

First of all, Paradise is a place for those who repented just before their death and accepted Jesus Christ to be saved, like the criminal who was hung on one side of Jesus. If you read Luke 23:39–43, you will find that two criminals were crucified on each side of Jesus. One criminal hurled insults at Jesus, but the second one rebuked the first, repented, and accepted Jesus as his Savior. Then, Jesus told the second criminal who repented that he was saved. "I tell you the truth," said Jesus, "today you will be with me in Paradise" (v. 43). This criminal just accepted Jesus as his Savior. He did neither cast his sins away nor live according to God's Word. Because he accepted the Lord just before he died, he did not have the time to learn about God's Word and act according to it.

You should realize that Paradise is for those who have accepted Jesus Christ, but have not done anything for the kingdom of God, like this criminal portrayed in Luke 23.

Yet, if you think, "I will accept the Lord just before I die so that I will be able to go to Paradise, which is so happy and beautiful, and cannot be compared to this earth," it is a wrong idea. God allowed the criminal on one side to be saved because He knew that the criminal had a good heart to love God till the end and not to forsake the Lord had he had more time to live.

However, not everybody can accept the Lord just before death, and the faith cannot be given in an instant. Therefore, you must realize the rarity of such a case in which the criminal on one side of Jesus was saved just before his death.

Also, people who receive shameful salvation still have much evil in their hearts even when they are saved, because they have lived as they liked. They will be grateful to God forever just for the fact that they are in Paradise and enjoy eternal life in heaven only by accepting Jesus Christ as their Savior, even though they have not done anything with faith on this earth.

Paradise is so different from New Jerusalem where God's throne is, but the fact that they did not go to hell but are saved alone makes them happy and joyful so much.

Lack of growth in spiritual faith

Second, even if people accepted Jesus Christ and have faith, but there was no growth in their faith, they receive the shameful salvation and go to Paradise. Not only the new believers but also the ones who believed for a long time have to go to Paradise if their faith stayed at the first level of faith all of the life.

Once, God allowed me to hear the confession of a believer who had been in faith for a long time, and is currently staying in the Waiting Place of heaven on the edge of Paradise.

He was born into a family that had not known God at all and worshiped idols. He began to live a Christian life later in his life. Yet, since he did not have true faith, he still lived within the boundaries of sin and lost the sight of one eye. He realized what true faith was after reading my testimonial book *Tasting Eternal Life Before Death*. He registered at our church and later went to heaven while he was leading a Christian life at church. I could hear his confession full of joy for being saved because he went to Paradise after suffering so much sorrow, pains, and diseases during his life on this earth:

I am so free and happy to come up here after taking off my flesh. I don't know why I tried to hold on to fleshly things. They were all meaningless. Holding on to fleshly things is so meaningless and useless since I have come up here after taking off the flesh.

In my life on the earth, there were times of joy and thanks, disappointment and despair. Here, when I look at myself within this comfort and happiness, I am reminded of the times when I tried to hold on to the meaningless life and keep myself in that meaningless life. But my soul lacks nothing now that I am in this comfortable place, and the fact that I can be in the place of salvation itself gives me a great joy.

I am very comfortable here in this place. I am so comfortable because I took off my flesh, and I take delight in that I have come to this peaceful place after the exhausting life on the earth. I didn't really know that it was such a happy thing to cast the flesh away, but I am so peaceful and joyful to have taken off the flesh and come to this place.

Not being able to see, not being able to walk, and not being able to do many other things were all a physical challenge to me at that time, but I am delightful and thankful after I have received the eternal life and come here because I feel I can be in this great place due to all those things.

Where I am is not the First Kingdom, the Second Kingdom, the Third Kingdom, or New Jerusalem. I'm only in Paradise, but I am so much thankful and joyful for being in Paradise.

My soul is satisfied with this.
My soul is praising with this.
My soul is happy with this.
My soul is thankful for this.

I am joyful and grateful because I finished the destitute and miserable life and came to enjoy this comfortable life.

Retrogressing in faith due to trials

Lastly, there are some people who have been faithful, but gradually become lukewarm in their faith for a variety of reasons, and barely received salvation.

A man who was an elder of my church served faithfully in many works of the church. So his faith seemed to be great on the outside, but one day he suddenly fell seriously ill. He could not even speak and came to receive my prayer. Instead of praying for the healing, I prayed for his salvation. At that time, his soul was suffering so much from the fear of the struggle between the angels who were trying to take him to heaven and the evil spirits who were trying to take him to hell. If he had had enough faith to be saved, the evil spirits would not have come to take him. So immediately I prayed to drive away the evil spirits, and prayed to God that He would receive this man. Right after the prayer, he gained comfort and shed tears. He repented just before he died and was barely saved.

Likewise, even if you received the Holy Spirit and were appointed the position of a deacon or an elder, it would be a shame in the eyes of God to live within sin. If you do not turn away from this kind of lukewarm spiritual life, the Holy Spirit in you gradually vanishes, and you will not be saved.

> I know your deeds, that you are neither cold nor hot. I wish you were either one or the other! So, because you are lukewarm—neither hot nor cold—I am about to spit you out of my mouth.
> —REVELATION 3:15–16

Therefore, you must realize that going to Paradise is such a shameful salvation and be more enthusiastic and vigorous about maturing your faith.

This man once had become healthy after receiving my prayer in the past and even his wife came back to life from the doorstep of death through my prayer. By listening to the words of life, his family who had many troubles became a happy family. Since then, he matured into a faithful worker of God through his endeavors and was faithful in his duties.

However, when the church faced a trial, he did not try to defend and protect the church but instead allowed his thoughts to be controlled by Satan. The words that came out of his mouth formed a great wall of sin between himself and God. Eventually, he could no longer be under God's protection, and was stricken by a serious disease.

As a worker of God, he should not have seen or listened to anything that was against truth and God's will, but instead, he wanted to listen to those things and spread them. God only had to turn His face away from him because he turned back from the great grace of God such as having been healed of a serious disease.

Therefore, his rewards crumbled down and he could not gain strength to pray. His faith retrogressed and finally reached the point where he could not even be certain of salvation. Luckily, God remembered his services to the church in the past. So the man could receive the shameful salvation since God gave him the grace to repent for what he had done before.

Full of gratitude for having been saved

So what kind of confessions would he make once he was saved and sent to Paradise? Because he was saved at the crossroad of heaven and hell, I could hear him confessing with true peace.

"I am saved like this. Even though I'm in Paradise, I am satisfied because I was freed from all fear and hardships. My spirit, which would have gone down to the darkness, has come into this beautiful and comfortable light."

How great his joy would be after he was freed from the fear of hell! Yet, since he was saved shamefully as an elder of the church, God let me hear his prayer of repentance while he was staying in the upper grave before he went to the Waiting Place in Paradise. He repented of his sins there as well, and thanked me for praying for him. He also made a vow to God to pray continually for me and the church he had served until he meets us again in heaven.

Since the beginning of the human cultivation on this earth, there have been more people who had the qualifications to go to Paradise than the total of all the people who are able to go to any other place in heaven. Those who are barely saved and go to Paradise are so thankful and happy about being able to enjoy the comfort and blessing of Paradise because they did not fall to hell despite not having led proper Christian lives on the earth.

However, the happiness in Paradise cannot even be compared to that of New Jerusalem, and it is also very different from the happiness of the next level, the First Kingdom of heaven. Therefore, you should realize that what is more important to God is not the years of your faith, but the attitude of your inner heart toward God and acting according to God's will.

Today, many people indulge and live in the sinful nature while professing that they have received the Holy Spirit. These people can barely receive shameful salvation and go to Paradise, or eventually fall to the death that is hell because the Holy Spirit in them will vanish.

Some nominal believers become arrogant after hearing and learning a great deal of God's Word, and judge and condemn other believers although they lead Christian lives for a long time. No matter how enthusiastic and faithful they are about God's ministries, it is of no use if they do not realize the evil in their hearts and cast their sins away.

Therefore, I pray in the name of the Lord that you, a child of God who has received the Holy Spirit, cast away your sins and all kinds of evil to strive to act only according to God's Word.

CHAPTER 7
THE FIRST KINGDOM OF HEAVEN

Everyone who competes in the games goes into strict training. They do it to get a crown that will not last; but we do it to get a crown that will last forever.

—1 CORINTHIANS 9:25

Paradise is the place for those who have accepted Jesus Christ but did not do anything with their faith. It is a much more beautiful and happier place than this earth. So, how much more beautiful the First Kingdom of heaven, the place for those who try to live according to God's Word, would be?

The First Kingdom is closer to God's throne than is Paradise, but there are many other better places in heaven. Yet, those who entered the First Kingdom would be satisfied with what they are given, and feel happy. It is like a goldfish being satisfied with staying in a fish bowl, not wanting anything more.

We will look in detail at what kind of place the First Kingdom of heaven is, which is one level higher than Paradise, and what kind of people enter there.

ITS BEAUTY AND HAPPINESS SURPASS PARADISE

Since Paradise is the place for those who have not done anything with their faith, there will be no personal property as rewards. From the First Kingdom and up, however, personal

111

properties such as houses and crowns are given as rewards.

In the First Kingdom, one lives in his or her own house and receives the crown that will last forever. It is such a glory in itself to possess one's own house in heaven, so each one in the First Kingdom feels happiness that cannot be compared to that of Paradise.

Personal houses decorated beautifully

Personal residences in the First Kingdom are not separate houses but resemble apartments or flats of this earth. However, they are not built with cement or bricks, but with beautiful heavenly materials like gold and jewels.

These houses do not have staircases, but only beautiful elevators. On this earth, you have to press the button, but in heaven they automatically go to the floor you want.

Among those who have been to heaven, there are those who testify that they saw apartments in heaven, and it is because they saw the First Kingdom among many heavenly places. These apartment-like houses have everything necessary for living, so there is no inconvenience at all.

For those who like music, there are musical instruments for them to play; and books for those who enjoy reading. Everybody has a personal space where he or she can rest, and it is really cozy.

In this way, in the First Kingdom surroundings are made according to the master's preferences. So it is a much more beautiful and happier place than Paradise, and full of joy and comfort that you can never experience on this earth.

Public gardens, lakes, and swimming pools

Since the houses in the First Kingdom are not single houses, there are public gardens, lakes, swimming pools, and golf courses. It is just like apartment complexes on this earth where the residents share public gardens, tennis courts, or swimming pools.

These public properties never get worn out or broken down, but angels always maintain the best condition. Angels help people with using those facilities, so there is no inconvenience even though they are public properties. There are no serving angels in Paradise, but people can get help from angels in the First Kingdom. So they feel a very different kind of joy and happiness here. Although there is no angel who belongs to any specific person, there are angels taking care of the facilities.

For example, if you want to have some fruit as you chat with your loved ones while sitting on the golden benches near the River of the Water of Life, the angels will immediately bring fruits and serve you politely. Because there are angels who help the children of God, the happiness and joy felt are so much different from those in Paradise.

The First Kingdom is superior to Paradise
Even the colors and scents of the flowers, and the brightness and beauty of animals' furs are different from those of Paradise. This is because God has provided everything according to the level of faith of the people in each place of heaven.

Even the people on this earth have different standards of beauty. Experts of flowers, for instance, will judge the beauty of even one flower based on many different criteria. In heaven, the scents of flowers in each dwelling place of heaven are different. Even within the same place, each flower has its unique scent.

God has provided the flowers in such a way that people in the First Kingdom would feel the best when they smell the scents of flowers. Of course, fruits have different tastes in different places of heaven. God has provided the colors and smell of each fruit according to the level of each dwelling place as well.

How do you prepare and serve when you receive an important guest? You will try to suit the taste of the guest in a way that would be to the utmost delight of your guest. Likewise, God has provided everything thoughtfully so that His children would be satisfied in all aspects.

WHAT KIND OF PEOPLE GO TO THE FIRST KINGDOM?

Paradise is the place of heaven for those who are at the first level of faith: saved by believing in Jesus Christ, but have not done anything for the kingdom of God. Then, what kind of people go to the First Kingdom of heaven above Paradise and enjoy the eternal life there?

People trying to act according to God's Word

The First Kingdom of heaven is the place for those who accepted Jesus Christ and tried to live according to God's Word. Those who have just accepted the Lord come to church on Sundays and listen to the Word of God, but they do not know what sin really is, why they have to pray, and why they have to cast their sins away. Likewise, the ones who are at the first level of faith have experienced the joy of the first love being born by water and the Holy Spirit, but do not realize what sin is and have not yet discovered their sins.

Yet, if you reach the second level of faith, you realize the sins and the righteousness with the help of the Holy Spirit. So you try to live according to God's Word, but you cannot do so immediately. It is just as a baby first learning to walk who repeats walking and falling down.

The First Kingdom is the place for these kinds of people, who try to live according to God's Word, and the crowns that will last forever will be given. Just as athletes have to play according to the rules of the game (2 Tim. 2:5), children of God have to fight the good fight of faith according to the truth. If you ignore the rules of the spiritual realm, which are God's law, like an athlete who does not play by the rules, you have a dead faith. Then you will not be considered as a participant and given any crown.

Still, for anyone in the First Kingdom, a crown is given because they have tried to live according to God's Word even though their deeds were not sufficient. However, it is still a shameful salvation. This is because they have not lived according to God's Word completely, even if they have faith to get to the First Kingdom.

Shameful salvation if the work is burned up

Then, what exactly is a "shameful salvation"? In 1 Corinthians 3:12–15 (NASB), you see that the work one has built up can either survive or be burned up:

> If any man builds on this foundation using gold, silver, costly stones, wood, hay or straw, his work will be shown for what it is, because the Day will bring it to light. It will be revealed with fire, and the fire will test the quality of each man's work. If what he has built survives, he will receive his reward. If it is burned up, he will suffer loss; he himself will be saved, but only as one escaping through the flames.

The "foundation" here refers to Jesus Christ and means whatever you build on this foundation, your work will be revealed through trials like fire.

On the one hand, the works of those who have faith like gold, silver, or jewels will remain even in fiery trials because they act according to God's Word. On the other hand, the works of those who have faith like wood, hay, or straw will be burned up when faced with fiery trials because they cannot act according to God's Word.

Therefore, to allocate these to the measures of faith, gold is the fifth (the highest), silver the fourth, jewels the third, wood the second, and hay is the first (and lowest) measure of faith. Wood and hay have life, and the faith like wood means that one has a living faith but it is weak. The straw, however, is dry and does not even have life, and it refers to those who do not have any faith.

Therefore, those who have no faith at all have nothing to do with salvation. The wood and the hay, whose works will be burned up by fiery trials, belong to the shameful salvation. God will recognize the faith of gold, silver, or jewels, but that of wood and hay, He cannot.

Faith without action is dead

Some might think, "I have been a Christian for a long time, so I must have passed the first level of faith, and I can at least go to the First Kingdom." Yet, if you truly have faith, you will obviously live according to God's Word. By the same token, if you break the law and do not cast your sins away, the First Kingdom, perhaps even Paradise, may be out of your reach.

The Bible asks you in James 2:14: "What good is it, my brothers, if a man claims to have faith but has no deeds? Can such faith save him?" If you have no deeds, you will not be saved. Faith without deeds is dead. So those who do not fight against sin cannot be saved because they are just like a man who received a mina and kept it laid away in a piece of cloth. (See Luke 19:20–26.)

The "mina" here stands for the Holy Spirit. God gives the Holy Spirit as a gift to those who open their hearts and accept Jesus Christ as their personal Savior. The Holy Spirit enables you to realize the sin, the righteousness, and the judgment, and helps you to be saved and go to heaven.

On the one hand, if you profess your belief in God but do not circumcise your heart by neither following the desire of the Holy Spirit nor acting according to the truth, then the Holy Spirit does not need to stay in your heart. On the other hand, if you cast your sins away and act according to God's Word with the help of the Holy Spirit, you can resemble the heart of Jesus Christ, who is the truth itself.

Therefore, the children of God who have received the Holy Spirit as a gift should sanctify their hearts and bear the fruits of the Holy Spirit to reach the perfect salvation.

Physically faithful but spiritually uncircumcised

God once revealed to me a member who had passed away and gone to the First Kingdom, and showed me the importance of faith accompanied by action. He served as a member of the finance department of the church for eighteen years without betraying in his heart. He was faithful in other works of God as well and was given the title of elder. He tried to bear fruits in numerous businesses and give glory to God, often asking himself, "How can I accomplish God's kingdom more greatly?"

Yet, he was not so successful because sometimes he disgraced God by not following the right path due to his fleshly thoughts and his heart that often sought his own good. Also, he would make dishonest remarks, get angry with other people, and disobey God's Word in many aspects.

In other words, because he was physically faithful but did not circumcise his heart—which is the most important thing—he remained at the second level of faith. Furthermore, if his financial and interpersonal problems had persisted, he would not have kept the faith but compromised with the unrighteousness. In the end, because the extent of the retrogression in his faith might not have allowed him even to enter Paradise, God called his soul at the best time.

Through spiritual communications after his death, he expressed his gratitude and repented many things. He repented for having hurt the feelings of ministers by not following the truth, for causing others to fall away, offending others, and not acting even after listening to the Word of God. He also said that he had always felt the pressure because he did not repent of his mistakes thoroughly when he was on this earth, but now he was happy because he could confess his mistakes.

Also, he said he was thankful that he did not end up in Paradise as an elder. It still was shameful to be in the First Kingdom as an elder, but he felt much better because the First Kingdom is much more glorious than Paradise.

Therefore, you should realize that the most important thing is circumcising your heart rather than physical faithfulness and titles.

God leads His children to better heaven through trials

Just as there must be hard training and many hours of practice for an athlete to win, you also have to face trials to go to better dwelling places in heaven. God allows trials for His children to lead them to better places in heaven, and the trials can be divided into three categories.

First, there are trials to cast away sins. In order to become God's true children, you have to fight against sins to the point of shedding your blood so that you can cast the sins away completely. Yet, God sometimes punishes His children because they do not cast sins away but continue to live in sins (Heb. 12:6). Just as parents sometimes punish their children to lead them to the right way, God sometimes allows His children to experience trials so they will be perfect.

Second, there are trials to make the proper vessel and give blessings. David, even when he was a young boy, saved his sheep by killing a bear or a lion that took his flock. He had such a great faith that he even killed Goliath, whom the whole Israelite army feared, with a sling and a stone by only relying on God. The reason he still had to face trials (i.e. being chased by King Saul) was because God allowed those trials to make David a big vessel and a great king.

Third, there are trials to put an end to idleness because people might stay away from God if they are at peace. For example, there are some people who are faithful in God's kingdom, and consequently receive financial blessings. They then stop praying and their enthusiasm for God cools down.

If God leaves them as they are, they might fall into death. So He allows trials for them to become clear-minded again.

You should cast away your sins, act righteously, and be proper vessels in the sight of God realizing the heart of God who allows the trials of faith. I hope you will fully receive the wondrous blessings that God has prepared for you.

Some might say, "I want to change, but it's not easy even though I try." Yet, they say such things not because it is truly difficult to change, but more because they lack the eagerness and passion to change deep inside their hearts.

If you really realize God's Word spiritually and try to change from your inner heart, you can change quickly because God gives you grace and strength to do so. The Holy Spirit, of course, helps you along the way as well. If you just know God's Word in your head only as a piece of knowledge but do not act accordingly, you are very likely to become proud and conceited, and it will be hard for you to be saved.

Therefore, I pray in the name of the Lord that you may not lose the passion and joy of your first love and keep on following the desire of the Holy Spirit so that you will possess a better place in heaven.

CHAPTER 8
THE SECOND KINGDOM OF HEAVEN

Be shepherds of God's flock that is under your care, serving as overseers—not because you must, but because you are willing, as God wants you to be; not greedy for money, but eager to serve; not lording it over those entrusted to you, but being examples to the flock. And when the Chief Shepherd appears, you will receive the crown of glory that will never fade away.

—1 PETER 5:2–4

On the one hand, no matter how much you hear about heaven, it will be of no use if you do not realize it in your heart because you cannot believe it. Just as a bird snatches a seed away sown along the path, the enemy Satan snatches away the Word about heaven from you (Matt. 13:19).

On the other hand, if you listen to the Word about heaven and grasp it, you can live a life of faith and hope and produce a crop yielding thirty, sixty, or a hundred times what was sown. Because you can act according to God's Word, you cannot only fulfill your duty but also be sanctified and faithful in all God's house. Then what kind of place is the Second Kingdom of heaven and what kind of people go there?

BEAUTIFUL PERSONAL HOUSE GIVEN TO EACH ONE

I have already explained that those who go to Paradise or the First Kingdom are saved shamefully because their works cannot remain when they are put through fiery trials. However, those who go to the Second Kingdom possess a kind of faith that passes fiery trials. They receive rewards that cannot be compared to those given in Paradise or the First Kingdom, according to God's righteousness, which rewards what was sown.

Therefore, if the happiness of the one who has gone to the First Kingdom is compared to the happiness of a goldfish in a fishbowl, the happiness of the one who has gone to the Second Kingdom may be compared to the happiness of a whale in the vast Pacific Ocean.

Now, let us look into the characteristics of the Second Kingdom, focusing on the houses and the life.

Single-story personal house given to each one

The houses of the First Kingdom are like apartments, but those of the Second Kingdom are completely independent single-story private buildings. The houses in the Second Kingdom cannot be compared to any beautiful houses or cottages or summer houses in this world. They are grand, beautiful, and are decorated fashionably with flowers and trees.

If you go to the Second Kingdom, you are given not only a house but also your most favorite object. If you want a swimming pool, you will be given one beautifully decorated with gold and all kinds of jewels. If you want a beautiful lake, you will be given a lake. If you want a ballroom, you will be given a ballroom as well. If you like taking a walk, you will be given a beautiful road full of wonderful flowers and plants around which many animals play.

However, even if you want to have all of the swimming pool, the lake, the ballroom, the road, and so forth, you can have only one thing you like the most. Because what people possess is different in the Second Kingdom, they visit each other's houses and enjoy together what they have.

If one who has a ballroom but not a swimming pool wants to swim, he can go to his neighbor who has a swimming pool and enjoy himself. In heaven, people serve each other, and they never feel bothered or reject any visitor. Instead, they would be more glad and happier. So if you want to enjoy something, you can visit your neighbors and enjoy what they have.

Likewise, the Second Kingdom is much better than the First Kingdom in all aspects. Of course, however, it cannot even be compared to New Jerusalem. They do not have angels who serve each child of God. The size, beauty, and splendor of the houses are so different, and the material, colors, and the brightness of the jewels that decorate the houses are so different, too.

Doorplate with beautiful and magnificent light

A house in the Second Kingdom is a single-story building with a doorplate. The doorplate indicates the owner of the house, and in some special cases it displays the name of the church that the owner served. It is written on the doorplate from which beautiful and magnificent lights brightly shine along with the name of the owner in heavenly letters that look like Arabic or Hebrew. So people in the Second Kingdom will say, "Oh! This is so-and-so's house who served such-and-such church!"

Why will the name of the church be specifically written? God does that so that the name will be the pride and glory to the members who served the church that will have built the grand sanctuary to receive the Lord at His Second Coming in the air.

Yet, houses in the Third Kingdom and New Jerusalem have no doorplates. There are not many people in either kingdom, and through the unique lights and aroma that come out from the houses, you can recognize to whom these houses belong.

Feeling sorry for not being fully sanctified

Some might wonder, "Won't it be inconvenient in heaven

since there are no private houses in Paradise, and in the Second Kingdom people can possess only one thing?" In heaven, however, there is nothing insufficient or inconvenient. People never feel uncomfortable because they live together. They are not stingy about sharing their possessions with others. They are just thankful for being able to share their possessions with others and consider it a source of great happiness.

Also, they neither feel sorry for having only one private possession nor become envious of things that others have. Instead, they are always deeply moved and thankful to God the Father for having given them much more than they deserve, and are always satisfied in unchanging joy and delight.

The only thing for which they feel sorry is the fact that they did not try hard enough and were not fully sanctified when they lived on this earth. They feel sorry and shameful to stand before God because they did not cast away all the evil within them. Even when they see those who have gone to the Third Kingdom or New Jerusalem, they do not envy them of their grand houses and glorious rewards, but feel sorry for not having made themselves completely sanctified.

Since God is righteous, He makes you reap what you sow, and rewards you according to what you have done. Therefore, He gives a place and rewards in heaven as you become sanctified and are faithful on this earth. Depending on the extent to which you live by God's Word, He will reward you accordingly and even handsomely.

If you lived completely according to God's Word, He will give you whatever you desire in heaven 100 percent. However, if you do not fully live according to God's Word, He will reward you according to only what you have done, but still abundantly.

Therefore, no matter which level of heaven you enter, you will be always thankful to God for giving you much more than what you have done on this earth, and live forever in happiness and joy.

The crown of glory

God, who rewards abundantly, gives a crown that will not perish to those in the First Kingdom. What kind of crown is given to those in the Second Kingdom?

Even though they were not fully sanctified, they gave glory to God by performing their duties. So they will receive the crown of glory. If you read 1 Peter 5:2–4, you see that the crown of glory is a reward given to those who set an example by living faithfully according to God's Word:

> Be shepherds of God's flock that is under your care, serving as overseers—not because you must, but because you are willing, as God wants you to be; not greedy for money, but eager to serve; not lording it over those entrusted to you, but being examples to the flock. And when the Chief Shepherd appears, you will receive the crown of glory that will never fade away.

The reason it says "the crown of glory that will never fade away" is because every crown in heaven is everlasting and never fades away. You will be able to realize that heaven is such a perfect place where everything is eternal and even one crown does not fade away.

WHAT KIND OF PEOPLE GO TO THE SECOND KINGDOM?

Around Seoul, the capital city of the Republic of Korea, there are satellite cities, and around those cities are small towns. In the same way, in heaven, around the Third Kingdom of heaven in which there is New Jerusalem, there are the Second Kingdom, the First Kingdom, and Paradise.

The First Kingdom is the place for those who are at the second level of faith who try to live according to God's Word. What kind of person goes to the Second Kingdom? A person at the third level of faith who can live according to God's

Word. Now let us consider what kind of people go to the Second Kingdom in detail.

The Second Kingdom: the place for people not completely sanctified

You can go to the Second Kingdom if you live according to God's Word and do your duties, but your heart is not yet fully sanctified.

If you are handsome, intelligent, and wise, you will obviously want your children to resemble you. In the same way, God, who is holy and perfect, wants His true children to resemble Him. He wants children who love Him and keep the commandments—who obey His commands because they love Him, and not out of a sense of duty. Just as you will do even a very difficult thing for someone you truly love, if you truly love God in your heart, you can keep any of His commandments with joy in your heart.

You will obey unconditionally with joy and thanks keeping what He tells you to keep, casting away what He tells you to cast away, not doing what He forbids you, and doing what He tells you to do. Yet, those who are at the third level of faith cannot act according to God's Word with complete joy and thanks in their hearts because they have not come into this level of love yet.

In the Bible, there are works of the flesh (Gal. 5:19–21), and desires of the flesh (Romans 8:5). When you act out the evil that is in your heart, it is called the works of the flesh. The natures of sin that you have in your heart that have not yet been shown externally are called the desires of the flesh.

Those at the third level of faith have already cast away all the works of the flesh that are outwardly visible, but they still have the desires of the flesh in their hearts. They keep what God tells them to keep, cast away what God tells them to cast away, do not do what God forbids them, and do what God tells them to do. Yet, the evil in their heart is not fully removed.

Likewise, if you perform your duty with your heart not completely sanctified, you can go to the Second Kingdom. "Sanctification" refers to the state in which you have cast away all kinds of evil and have only goodness in your heart.

For example, let us say there is a person you hate. Now, you have listened to the Word of God, saying, "Do not hate," and tried not to hate him. As a result, you do not hate him now. However, if you do not truly love him in your heart, you are not yet sanctified.

Therefore, to grow to the fourth measure of faith from the third, it is crucial to have the effort to cast sins away up to the point of shedding blood.

People having fulfilled the duty by God's grace

The Second Kingdom is the place for those who have not accomplished complete sanctification of their hearts but have fulfilled their duties given from God. Let us consider the kind of people who go to the Second Kingdom by looking at the case of a member who passed away while she was serving Manmin Joong-ang Church.

She came with her husband to Manmin Joong-ang Church in the year it was founded. She had been suffering from a serious disease but was healed after she received my prayer, and her family members became believers. They matured in their faith, and she became a senior deaconess, her husband an elder, and their children grew up and are serving the Lord as a minister, a pastor's wife, and a praise missionary.

However, she failed to cast away every kind of evil and carry out her duty properly, but she repented by God's grace, completed her duty well, and passed away. God let me know that she would stay in the Second Kingdom of heaven and allowed me to have communication with her in spirit.

When she went to heaven, the thing for which she felt most sorry is the fact that she had not cast away all her sins to be completely sanctified, and the fact that she had not really done any confession of thanks from her heart to her shepherd who had prayed for her to be healed and led her with love.

Also, she had thought that considering what she had accomplished with her faith, how she served the Lord, and the words that she spoke with her mouth, she could have only gone to the First Kingdom. However, when she did not have much time left on this earth, through the loving prayer of her shepherd and her deeds that pleased God, her faith quickly grew and she was able to enter the Second Kingdom.

Her faith actually grew very rapidly before she passed away. She concentrated on praying and delivered thousands of church newsletters around her neighborhood. She did not look after herself, but only served the Lord faithfully.

She told me about her house in which she was going to live in heaven. She said that, though it is a single-story building, it is decorated so wonderfully with beautiful flowers and trees, and it is so large and magnificent that it cannot be compared to any house on this earth.

Of course, compared to houses in the Third Kingdom or New Jerusalem, it is like a straw-roofed house, but she was so thankful and satisfied because she did not deserve to have it. She wanted to convey the following message to her family so that they would go to New Jerusalem.

> Heaven is divided so accurately. The glory and the light are so different in each place, so I urge and encourage them again and again to enter New Jerusalem. I would like to tell my family members who are still on the earth how shameful it is not to have cast away all the sins when we meet our Father God in heaven. The rewards God gives to those who go to New Jerusalem and the grandeur of the houses are all enviable, but I would like to tell them how sorry and shameful it is not to have cast away all kinds of evil before God. I would like to convey this message to my family members so that they will cast

away all kinds of evil and enter the glorious positions of New Jerusalem.

Therefore, I urge you to realize how precious and valuable it is to sanctify your heart and to devote your daily life for the kingdom and righteousness of God with the hope for heaven, so that you will be able to forcefully advance toward New Jerusalem.

People faithful in everything but disobeying due to their own wrong framework of righteousness

Now, let us have a look at the case of another member who loved the Lord and did her duty faithfully, but could not go to the Third Kingdom because of some deficiencies in her faith.

She came to Manmin Joong-ang Church for her husband's disease and became a very active member. Her husband was carried to the church on a stretcher, but his pain was gone and he came to stand up and walk. Imagine how grateful and joyful she must have been! She was always thankful to God who had healed her husband's disease and her ministering pastor who prayed with love. She was always faithful. She prayed for the kingdom of God and prayed with thanks to her shepherd at all times when she was walking, sitting or standing, and even when she was cooking.

Also, because she loved the brothers and sisters in Christ, she comforted others rather than being comforted, and she encouraged and took care of other believers. She only wanted to live according to God's Word and tried to cast away all her sins to the point of shedding blood. She never envied or longed for worldly possessions but only concentrated on preaching the gospel to her neighbors.

Because she was so faithful to God's kingdom, my heart was inspired with the Holy Spirit at the sight of her loyalty and asked her to take the duty of my church service. I had the faith that if she performed her duty faithfully, then all her family members including her husband would come to have spiritual faith.

However, she could not obey because she looked at her circumstances and was consumed by her fleshly thoughts. A little later she passed away. I was heartbroken, and while I was praying to God, I could hear her confession through spiritual communication.

> Even if I repent and repent of not obeying the shepherd, the clock cannot be turned back. So I am only praying for the kingdom of God and for the shepherd more and more. One thing I have to tell my dear brothers and sisters is that what the shepherd proclaims is the will of God. It is the greatest sin to disobey God's will, and along with it anger is the greatest sin. Because of this, people face difficulties, and I was commended for not getting angry, but humbling my heart, and striving to obey with my whole heart. I have become a person who blows the trumpet of the Lord. The day when I will receive dear brothers and sisters is coming soon. I just hope earnestly that my dear brothers and sisters are clear-minded and lack nothing so that they will also look forward to this day.

She confessed much more than this, and told me that the reason she could not go to the Third Kingdom was because of her disobedience.

> I had a few things that I disobeyed until I came to this kingdom. I sometimes said, "No, No, No," while I was listening to the messages. I did not do my duty properly. Because I thought I would carry out my duty when my circumstances got better, I used my fleshly thoughts. It was such a big mistake in the sight of God.

She also said she had envied ministers and those who took care of the church finance whenever she saw them, thinking that their rewards in heaven would be so great.

130

Yet, she confessed that when she went to heaven, that was really not often the case.

> No! No! No! Only those who act according to God's will receive great rewards and blessings. If the leaders make a mistake, it is a much greater sin than an ordinary member making a mistake. They have to pray more. The leaders have to be more faithful. They have to teach better. They must have the ability to discern. That is why it is written in one of the four Gospels that a blind man leads another blind man. This is the meaning of the word, "Let not many of you become teachers." One will be blessed if he tries the best in his position. Now, the day when we will meet each other as God's children in the eternal kingdom is coming soon. Therefore, everybody should cast away all the works of the flesh, become righteous, and have the proper qualifications as the Lord's bride without any shame when they stand before God.

Therefore, you should realize how important it is to obey not from the sense of duty but because of the joy in your inner heart and your love for God, and to sanctify your heart. Moreover, you should not be merely a churchgoer, but look at yourself to determine what kind of heavenly kingdom you can enter if the Father called your soul now.

You should try to be faithful in all your duties and live according to God's Word, so that you will be completely sanctified and have all the necessary qualifications ready to enter New Jerusalem.

First Corinthians 15:41 tells you that the glory each person receives in heaven will be different. It says, "The sun has one kind of splendor, the moon another and the stars another; and star differs from star in splendor."

All those who are saved will enjoy eternal life in heaven. Yet, some will stay in Paradise while some will be in New Jerusalem, all according to their measure of faith. The difference in the glory is so great that it is inexpressible.

Therefore, I pray in the name of the Lord that you do not remain in the faith merely to be saved, but as a farmer who sold all his possessions to buy the field and dig up the treasure, live according to God's Word completely and cast away all kinds of evil so that you will enter New Jerusalem and stay in the glory that shines there like the sun.

Chapter 9
The Third Kingdom of Heaven

Blessed is the man who perseveres under trial,
because when he has stood the test, he will receive
the crown of life that God has promised to those
who love him.

—James 1:12

God is spirit, and He is goodness, light, and love itself. That is why He wants His children to cast away all sin and all kinds of evil. Jesus, who came to this world in human flesh, has no blemish because He is God Himself. So what kind of person should you be to become a bride who will receive the Lord?

To become God's true child and a bride of the Lord who will share true love with God eternally, you have to resemble the holy heart of God and sanctify yourself by casting away all kinds of evil.

The Third Kingdom of heaven, which is the place for God's children who are holy and resemble God's heart, is so much different from the Second Kingdom. Because God hates evil and loves goodness so much, He treats His children who are sanctified in a very special way. Then, what kind of place is the Third Kingdom and how much do you have to love God to go there?

Angels Serve Each Child of God

Houses in the Third Kingdom are much more magnificent and brilliant than the single-story houses in the Second Kingdom beyond comparison. They are decorated with so many kinds of jewels and have all the facilities that the owners would like to have. Moreover, from the Third Kingdom on, angels who serve each one will be given, and they will love and adore the master and serve him or her with only the very best things.

Angels serving privately

It says in Hebrews 1:14 "Are not all angels ministering spirits sent to serve those who will inherit salvation?" Angels are purely spiritual beings. They resemble human beings in shape as one of God's creations, but they do not have flesh and bones, and have nothing to do with marriage or death. They do not have personalities like human beings, but their knowledge and power are much greater than those of human beings (2 Pet. 2:11).

As Hebrews 12:22 speaks of thousands upon thousands of angels, there are countless angels in heaven. God has made the order and ranks among the angels, assigned them different tasks, and given them different authorities according to the task.

So there are differentiations among the angels, such as angel, heavenly host, and archangel. For instance, Gabriel, who serves as a civil official, comes to you with answers to your prayers or God's plans and revelations (Dan. 9:21–23; Luke 1:19, 26–27). Archangel Michael, who is like a military officer, is the minister of the heavenly army. He controls the battles against the evil spirits, and sometimes he himself breaks the battle lines of the darkness (Dan. 10:13–14, 21; Jude 1:9; Rev. 12:7–8).

Among these angels, there are angels that serve their masters privately. In Paradise, the First Kingdom, and the Second Kingdom there are angels who sometimes help the children of God, but there is not any angel who serves the master privately. There are only the angels who take care of the grass, or the flower roads, or public facilities to make sure that there is no inconvenience, and there are angels that deliver God's messages.

But, for those who are in the Third Kingdom or New Jerusalem, private angels are rewarded because the people there have loved God and pleased Him so much. Also, the number of angels given will be different according to the extent to which one resembles God and has pleased Him with obedience.

If one has a house of great size in New Jerusalem, countless angels will be given because it means the owner resembles the heart of God and has led many people to salvation. There will be angels who take care of the house, some angels who take care of facilities and things that are given as rewards, and other angels who serve the master privately. There will be just so many angels.

If you go to the Third Kingdom, you will not only have angels who serve you privately but also angels who take care of your house and angels who usher and help the visitors. You will be so thankful to God if you could enter the Third Kingdom because God lets you reign forever while being served by the angels whom He gives you as eternal rewards.

Magnificent multiple-story personal house

The houses in the Third Kingdom that are decorated with beautiful flowers and trees with wonderful aroma have gardens and lakes. In the lakes are many fish, and people can have conversations with them and share love with them. Also, angels play beautiful music and people can praise Father God along with them.

Unlike Second Kingdom residents who are allowed to have only one favorite object or facility, people in the Third Kingdom can possess anything they want such as a golf course, a swimming pool, a lake, a passage for walking, a ballroom, and so on. Therefore, they do not have to go to neighbors' houses to enjoy something they do not have, and they can enjoy themselves anytime they want.

Houses in the Third Kingdom are multiple-story buildings

and are magnificent, grand, and large in size. They are decorated so beautifully that no billionaire in this world could imitate them.

By the way, no house in the Third Kingdom has a doorplate. People just know whose house it is even without a doorplate, because the unique scent that expresses the clean and beautiful heart of the master flows from the house. Houses in the Third Kingdom have different scents and different brightness of the lights. The more the master resembles the heart of God, the more beautiful and brighter the scent and the light are.

Also, in the Third Kingdom, pet animals and birds are given, and they are much more beautiful, brilliant, and lovely than the ones in the First or the Second Kingdom. Moreover, the cloud automobiles are given to be used publicly, and people can travel all around the limitless heaven as much as they want.

As it is explained, in the Third Kingdom people can have and do everything they want. The life in the Third Kingdom would be beyond imagination.

The crown of life

In Revelation 2:10, there is a promise of "the crown of life" that will be given to those who have been faithful even to the point of death for the kingdom of God:

> Do not be afraid of what you are about to suffer. I tell you, the devil will put some of you in prison to test you, and you will suffer persecution for ten days. Be faithful, even to the point of death, and I will give you the crown of life.

The phrase "being faithful even to the point of death" here refers to not only being faithful with the faith of becoming a martyr, but also not compromising with the world, and becoming completely holy by casting away all sins up to the point of shedding blood. God rewards all those who enter the Third Kingdom with the crowns of life because they have been faithful even to the point of death and have overcome all kinds of trials and hardships (James 1:12).

When the people in the Third Kingdom visit New Jerusalem, they put a round mark on the right edge of the crown of life. When people in Paradise, the First Kingdom, or the Second Kingdom visit New Jerusalem, they put a sign on the left side of the chest. You can see the glory is different for the people in the Third Kingdom in this way.

However, the people in New Jerusalem are under the special care of God, so they need no sign to distinguish themselves. They are treated in a very exceptional manner as God's true children.

Houses in New Jerusalem

Houses in the Third Kingdom are quite different from the houses in New Jerusalem in size, beauty, and glory.

First of all, if you say the size of the smallest house in New Jerusalem is 100, the smallest house in the Third Kingdom is 60. For example, if the smallest house in New Jerusalem is 100,000 square feet, the smallest house in the Third Kingdom would be 60,000 square feet.

Yet, the size of individual houses varies because it entirely depends on how much the master worked to save as many souls as they could and to build God's church. As Jesus says in Matthew 5:5, "Blessed are the meek, for they will inherit the earth," depending on the number of souls the owner of the house leads to heaven with a meek heart, the size of the house in which he or she will live will be accordingly determined.

So there are many houses more than tens of thousands of square feet in the Third Kingdom and in New Jerusalem, but even the biggest house in the Third Kingdom is much smaller than the ones in New Jerusalem. In addition to the size, the shape, beauty, and the jewels for decoration are vastly different as well.

In New Jerusalem, there are not only the twelve jewels for

the foundation, but also many other beautiful jewels. There are jewels unimaginably big with such beautiful colors. There are just so many kinds of jewels that you cannot name them all, and some of them shine like double or even triple overlapped lights.

Of course, there are many jewels in the Third Kingdom. However, despite their variety, jewels of the Third Kingdom cannot be compared to those in New Jerusalem. There is no jewel that shines like double or triple lights in the Third Kingdom. The jewels in the Third Kingdom have much more beautiful lights compared to the ones in the First or Second Kingdom, but there are only simple and basic jewels, and even the same kind of jewel is less beautiful than the one in New Jerusalem. That is why people in the Third Kingdom staying outside New Jerusalem, which is full of God's glory, look at it and long to be there forever more.

"Only if I tried a little harder and was more faithful in all God's house..."

"Only if the Father calls my name once..."

"Only if I am invited once more..."

There is an unimaginable amount of happiness and beauty in the Third Kingdom, but they cannot be compared to those of New Jerusalem.

WHAT KIND OF PEOPLE GO TO THE THIRD KINGDOM?

When you open your heart and accept Jesus Christ as your personal Savior, the Holy Spirit comes and teaches you about the sin, the righteousness, and the judgment, and makes you realize the truth. When you obey the Word of God, cast away all kinds of evil and become sanctified, you are at the state of your soul getting along well—at the fourth level of faith.

Ones who reach the fourth level of faith love God so much and are loved by God and enter the Third Kingdom. Then, what specific kind of person has the faith with which he can enter the Third Kingdom?

Being sanctified by casting away all kinds of evil

During times of the Old Testament, people did not receive the Holy Spirit. Thus, they could not cast away the sins that were deep inside the heart with their own strength. That is why they performed the physical circumcision, and unless the evil appeared in action, they did not consider it a sin. Even if one had the thought of murdering someone, it was not considered a sin so long as the thought did not result in action. Only when the thought was carried out, was it considered as a sin.

However, during times of the New Testament and today, if you accept the Lord Jesus Christ, the Holy Spirit comes into your heart. Unless your heart is sanctified, you cannot enter the Third Kingdom. It is because you can circumcise your heart with the help of the Holy Spirit.

Therefore, you can enter the Third Kingdom only when you cast away all kinds of evil such as hatred, adultery, greed and the like, and then become sanctified. Then, what kind of person has a sanctified heart? He is the one who has the kind of spiritual love described in 1 Corinthians 13:1–8, the nine fruits of the Holy Spirit in Galatians 5:22–23, and the Beatitudes in Matthew 5:1–12, and who resembles the holiness of the Lord.

Of course, it does not mean he is at the same level with the Lord. No matter how much a human being casts away his sins and becomes sanctified, his level is so much different from God, who is the origin of light.

Therefore, in order to sanctify your heart, you first have to make the good soil in your heart. In other words, you should make your heart good soil by not doing what the Bible tells you not to do and casting away what the Bible tells you to cast away. Only then, will you be able to bear good fruits as the seeds are sown. Just as a farmer sows the seeds after he clears the land, the seeds sown in you sprout, bloom, and bear fruit after doing what God tells you to do and keeping what He tells you to keep.

Therefore, sanctification refers to a state when one gets cleansed from the original and self-committed sins by the works of the Holy Spirit after he is born again by the water and the Holy Spirit by believing in the redeeming power of Jesus Christ. Being forgiven of your sins by believing in the blood of Jesus Christ is different from casting away the natures of sin within you with the help of the Holy Spirit by praying fervently and intermittently with fasting.

Accepting Jesus Christ and becoming God's child does not mean that all your sins in your heart are removed completely. You still have evil such as hatred, pride, and the like in you, and that is why the process of finding out the evil by listening to the Word of God and fighting against it to the point of shedding blood is vital (Heb. 12:4).

This is how you cast away the works of the flesh and progress towards sanctification. The state in which you have thrown out not only the acts of sinful nature but also the desires of the flesh in your heart is the fourth level of faith, the state of sanctification.

Why did God allow a severe trial to Job?

Through James 1:12, you can see that God sometimes allows trials and leads you to accomplish sanctification.

> Blessed is the man who perseveres under trial, because when he has stood the test, he will receive the crown of life that God has promised to those who love him.

Job in the Old Testament was righteous enough to be recognized by God as a man who was blameless and upright, and who feared God and shunned evil (Job 1:1).

One day, he encountered a trial. He lost all his children and all his wealth. Job did not complain at all, but he only gave thanks and glory to God.

When the trial continued, however, he began to complain before God, saying, "I have been righteous and revered God. Why then is God giving me this pain?"

Then, why did God allow this trial to Job, who was said to be a righteous man? Just like a craftsman would want his precious jewel to be made perfect and pure, God wanted to mold Job into a much more beautiful vessel by this trial.

Even the blameless and upright Job had sins in his nature of which he had not known. So God allowed the trial to take place in order to sanctify him completely. After Job was approved, God blessed him twice as much as he had before.

Sanctified only after casting off sins in nature

What, then, are sins in one's nature? They are all the sins that have been passed down through the seeds of life of one's parents since Adam's disobedience. For example, you can find that a baby who is not even a year old has an evil mind. Although his mother has never taught him any evil such as hatred or jealousy, he will get angry and do evil actions if his mother gives her breast to a neighbor's baby. And he may try to push away the neighbor's baby and would start to cry, filled with anger, if the baby does not go away from his mother.

Likewise, the reason even a baby shows acts of evil, although he has not learned any of it before, is because there is sin in his nature. Also, self-committed sins are the sins revealed in physical actions following the sinful desires of the heart.

Of course, if you are sanctified from the original sin, it is obvious that your self-committed sins will be thrown away because the root of sins is removed. Therefore, spiritual rebirth is the beginning of sanctification, and sanctification the perfection of rebirth. Therefore, if you are born again, I hope you will live a successful Christian life to accomplish sanctification.

If you really want to be sanctified and recover the lost image of God, and try your best, then you will be able to cast away sins in your nature by the grace and strength of God and with the help of the Holy Spirit. I hope you will resemble God's holy heart as He urges you, "Be holy, because I am holy" (1 Pet. 1:16).

People with the faith of martyrdom

Just as the one who loves God so much and becomes sanctified in his heart can enter the Third Kingdom, you can enter at least the Third Kingdom if you have the faith of martyrdom with which you can sacrifice everything, even your life, for God.

The members of early Christian churches who kept the faith until they were beheaded, eaten by the lions in the Coliseum in Rome, or burnt will receive the reward of a martyr in heaven. It is not easy to become a martyr under such severe persecutions and threats.

Around you, there are many people who do not keep the day of the Lord holy or who neglect their God-given duty because of their desire for money. These kinds of people, who cannot obey such a small thing, can never keep their faith in a life-threatening situation, much less become a martyr.

What kinds of people have the faith of martyrs? The ones who have upright and unchanging hearts like Daniel's from the Old Testament. However, those who have double minds and seek their own good, compromising with the world, have very little chance of becoming martyrs.

Those who can truly become martyrs must have unchanging hearts like Daniel's. He kept the righteousness of faith knowing well that he would go into the lions' den. He kept his faith until even the last moment when he was thrown into the lions' den by the trick of the evil people. Daniel never went away from the truth because his heart was clean and pure.

It is the same with Stephen from the New Testament. He was stoned to death while he was preaching the gospel of the Lord. Stephen was also a sanctified man who could pray even for those who were stoning him despite his innocence. So how much would the Lord love him? He will walk with the Lord forever in heaven, and his beauty and glory will be tremendous. Therefore, you should realize that the most important thing is to accomplish the righteousness and sanctification of the heart.

There are very few who have the true faith today. Even Jesus asked, "When the Son of Man comes, will he find faith on the earth?"(Luke 18:8). How precious would you be in the eyes of God if you become a sanctified child by keeping the faith and casting away all kinds of evil even in this world that is full of sins?

Therefore, I pray in the name of the Lord that you will pray fervently and quickly make your heart sanctified; looking forward to the glory and rewards that God the Father will give you in heaven.

CHAPTER 10
NEW JERUSALEM

I saw the Holy City, the new Jerusalem, coming
down out of heaven from God, prepared as a bride
beautifully dressed for her husband.

—Revelation 21:2

In New Jerusalem, which is the most beautiful place in
heaven and full of God's glory, there are God's throne, the
castles of the Lord and the Holy Spirit, and houses of the
people who pleased God so much with the highest level of
faith.

Houses in New Jerusalem are being prepared most beautifully
the way the would-be masters of the houses want them to be.
In order to enter New Jerusalem, which is clear and beautiful as
crystal, and share true love with God forever, you must not only
resemble God's holy heart but also do your duty completely like
the Lord Jesus did.

Now, what kind of place is New Jerusalem, and what kinds
of people go there?

PEOPLE IN NEW JERUSALEM SEE GOD FACE-TO-FACE

New Jerusalem, also called the heavenly Holy City, is as beautiful as a bride who has prepared herself for her husband.
People there have the privilege of meeting God face-to-face
because His throne is there.

It is also called "the city of glory" because you will receive
the glory from God forever when you enter New Jerusalem.

The wall of the city is made of jasper, and the city pure gold, as pure as glass. There are three gates on each of the four sides of the wall—north, south, east, and west—and there is an angel to guard each gate. The twelve foundations of the city are made of twelve different kinds of jewels.

Twelve Pearl Gates of New Jerusalem

Then, why are twelve gates of New Jerusalem made of pearls? A shell endures for a long time and puts in all its juice to make one pearl. In the same way, you must cast away sins by fighting against them up to the point of shedding blood and be faithful to the point of death before God in endurance and self-control. God has made the gates of pearls because you have to overcome your circumstances with joy to perform your God-given duties even though you are going the narrow way.

So when a person who enters New Jerusalem passes the pearl gate, he sheds tears of joy and excitement. He gives all inexpressible thanks and glory to God who has led him to New Jerusalem.

Also, what is the reason God made the twelve foundations of twelve different jewels? It is because the combination of the significance of the twelve jewels is the heart of the Lord and the Father. Therefore, you should realize the spiritual meanings of each jewel and accomplish the spiritual meanings in your heart to enter New Jerusalem. I will explain in detail those meanings in *Heaven II: Filled With God's Glory.*

Houses in New Jerusalem in perfect unity and variety

Houses in New Jerusalem are like castles in their size and magnificence. Each is unique according to the preferences of the owner, and is in perfect unity and variety. Also, various colors and lights coming out from the jewels make you feel the beauty and glory beyond expression.

People can recognize to whom each house belongs by

just looking at it. They can understand how much its owner pleased God when he or she was on earth by looking at the light of glory and the jewels that decorate the house.

For example, the house of a person who became a martyr on this earth will have decorations and records about the owner's heart and achievements until the martyrdom. The record is carved on a golden plate and shines so brightly. It would read, "The owner of this house became a martyr and fulfilled the will of the Father on the __th day of the __th month in the year____."

Even from the gate, people can see the bright light that comes out from the golden plate where the owner's achievements are recorded, and all those who see it will bow. Martyrdom is such a great glory and reward, and it is a pride and joy of God.

Since there is no evil in heaven, people automatically bow their heads according to the rank and the depth in which one is beloved by God. Also, just as people present a plaque of thanks or meritorious service to celebrate great achievements, God also gives a plaque to each one in celebration for giving Him glory. You can see that the scents and the lights differ according to the kinds of plaques.

Furthermore, God provides in people's houses something with which they can remember their lives on this earth by. Of course, even in heaven you can watch events of the past on this earth on something like a television.

The crown of gold or righteousness

If you enter New Jerusalem, you will basically be given your personal house and the crown of gold, and the crown of righteousness will be awarded according to your deeds. This is the most glorious and beautiful crown in heaven.

God Himself rewards the crowns of gold to those who enter New Jerusalem. Around the throne of God are twenty-four elders with the crowns of gold:

> Surrounding the throne were twenty-four other thrones,
> and seated on them were twenty-four elders. They were
> dressed in white and had crowns of gold on their heads.
>
> —REVELATION 4:4

"Elders" here do not refer to the title given in earthly churches, but those who are right in the sight of God and recognized by God. They are sanctified and have accomplished the sanctuary in their hearts as well as the visible sanctuary.

"Accomplishing the sanctuary in the heart" refers to becoming a person of spirit by casting away all kinds of evil. Accomplishing the visible sanctuary means performing the duties on this earth completely.

The number "twenty-four" stands for all people who have entered the gate of salvation by faith, like the twelve tribes of Israel, and become sanctified like the twelve disciples of Jesus the Lord. Therefore, "twenty-four elders" refer to the children of God who are recognized by God and are faithful in all God's house.

Therefore, those who have faith like gold that never changes will receive the crowns of gold, and those who long for the Lord's appearing like the apostle Paul will receive the crown of righteousness.

> Now there is in store for me the crown of righteousness,
> which the Lord, the righteous Judge, will award to me on
> that day—and not only to me, but also to all who have
> longed for his appearing.
>
> —2 TIMOTHY 4:8

Those who long for the Lord's appearing will obviously live within the light and the truth, and will become well-prepared vessels and the Lord's brides. Therefore, they will receive the crowns accordingly.

The apostle Paul was not overwhelmed by any persecution or hardship, but only tried to expand God's kingdom and accomplish His righteousness in all he did. He revealed God's glory greatly wherever he went with his labor and perseverance. That is why God has prepared the crown of righteousness for the apostle Paul. And He will give it to all who long for the Lord's appearing like he did.

Every desire in their hearts will be fulfilled

What you had in mind on this earth—what you loved to do but gave up for the Lord—God will give you back all these things as beautiful rewards in New Jerusalem.

Therefore, houses in New Jerusalem have everything you wanted to have, so that you can do everything you wanted to do. Some houses have lakes so that the owners can go boating and some have a forest in which they can take a walk. People may also enjoy talking to their dear ones at a tea table at the corner of a beautiful garden. There are houses with meadows covered with grass and flowers, so that people can walk or sing praises with various birds and beautiful animals.

In this way, God has made in heaven everything you wanted to have on this earth without missing a single object. How deeply will you be moved when you see all these things God has provided for you with great care?

Actually, being able to enter New Jerusalem itself is a source of happiness. You will live in unchanging happiness, glory, and beauty forever. You will be full of joy and excitement when you look at the ground, when you look at the sky, or wherever else you look. People feel peaceful, comfortable, and safe just by staying in New Jerusalem because God has made it for His children whom He truly loves, and every corner of it is filled with His love.

In New Jerusalem, love for God the Father is like a fountain and you will be filled with everlasting happiness, thanks, and joy. Whatever you do—whether you walk, rest, play, eat, or talk to other people—you will be filled with happiness and joy. Trees, flowers, grass, and even animals are all lovely, and you will feel the glory with magnificence from the walls of the castle, decorations, and the facilities in the house.

Seeing God face-to-face

In New Jerusalem, where there is the highest level of glory, beauty, and happiness, you can meet God face-to-face and walk with the Lord, and can live with your loved ones forever and ever. You will also be admired not only by angels and heavenly hosts, but also by all people in heaven. Furthermore, your personal angels will serve you like serving a king, meeting all your wants and needs perfectly. If you want to fly in the sky, your personal cloud automobile will come and stop right in front of your feet. As soon as you get in the cloud automobile, you can fly it in the sky as much as you want, or you can drive it on the ground.

So if you enter New Jerusalem, you can see God face-to-face, live with your dear ones eternally, and all your desires will be given in an instant. You can have everything you want, and also be treated like a prince or a princess in a fairy tale.

Participating in New Jerusalem banquets

In New Jerusalem, there are always banquets. Sometimes the Father hosts the banquets, or sometimes the Lord or the Holy Spirit does. You can feel the joy of heavenly life very well through these banquets. You can feel the abundance, freedom, beauty, and joy at a glance in these banquets.

When you participate in the banquets held by the Father, you will put on the best dress and decorations, eat and drink the best food and beverages. You will also enjoy charming and beautiful music, praises, and dances. You can watch angels dancing, or sometimes you yourself can dance to please God.

Angels are more beautiful and perfect in techniques, but God is more pleased with the aroma of His children who know His heart and love Him from their hearts.

Those who served for the worship service offered to God on this earth will also serve in those banquets to make it more blissful, and those who praised God with singing, dancing, and playing instruments will do the same at the heavenly banquets. You will put on a soft clothes, a wonderful crown, and decorations of jewels with such brilliant lights. Also, you will be riding in a cloud automobile or on a golden wagon escorted by angels to attend banquets. Isn't your heart pounding for joy and expectations from simply imagining all this?

Cruising festival on the Sea of Glass

In the beautiful sea of heaven flows a body of clear and clean water that is like a crystal without any blemish or spot. The water of the blue sea has gentle waves by breeze, and it shines brightly. Many kinds of fish swim in the water that is so transparent, and when people approach them, they welcome them by moving their fins and confessing their love.

Also, there are groups of corals of many colors that sway. Every time they move, they give out the lights of those beautiful colors. How wondrous the sight is! There are many small islands in the sea, and they look marvelous. Moreover, cruise ships like the *Titanic* sail around, and there are banquets aboard the ships as well. These ships are equipped with all kinds of facilities including comfortable accommodations, bowling alleys, swimming pools, and ballrooms so that people can enjoy whatever they want. Just imagine all the festivals on these ships, which are grander and more wonderfully decorated than any luxurious cruise ship on this earth, with the Lord and your loved ones. It will be such a great joy.

WHAT KIND OF PEOPLE GO TO NEW JERUSALEM?

Those who have faith like gold, who long for the Lord's appearing, and who prepare themselves as brides of the Lord will enter New Jerusalem. Then, what kind of person do you have to be in order to enter New Jerusalem, which is clear and beautiful as crystal and full of God's grace?

People with faith to please God

New Jerusalem is the place for those who are at the fifth level of faith—those who not only completely sanctified their hearts but also were faithful in all God's house.

Faith that pleases God is the kind of faith with which God is thoroughly satisfied so that He wants to fulfill requests and desires of His children before they ask.

How, then, can you please God? I will give you an example. Let us say a father comes back home from his work and tells his two sons that he is thirsty. The first son, who knows that his father likes soda, brings a glass of Coke or Sprite for his father. Also, the son gives his father a massage for his comfort, even though the father did not ask for one.

On the other hand, the second son just brings a glass of water to his father and goes back to his room. Now, which of the two sons pleased his father more, understanding the heart of the father?

Instead of the son who just brought a glass of water simply to obey the father's word, the father must have been more pleased with the son who brought a glass of soda he liked and gave him a massage for which he had not asked.

In the same way, the difference between those who enter the Third Kingdom and New Jerusalem lies in the extent to which people pleased the heart of God the Father and were faithful according to the Father's will.

People of whole spirit with the heart of the Lord

Those who have the faith that pleases God fill their hearts only with the truth, and are faithful in all God's house. Being faithful in all God's house means performing the duties more than one is expected to do with the faith of the Christ Himself, who obeyed the will of God to the point of death, not caring about His own life.

Therefore, those who are faithful in all God's house do not do the works with their own mind and thoughts, but only with the heart of the Lord, the spiritual heart. Paul writes in Philippians 2:6–7 that Jesus "being in very nature God, did not consider equality with God something to be grasped, but made himself nothing, taking the very nature of a servant, being made in human likeness," and obeyed to the point of death to accomplish God's will. In turn, God lifted Him up, gave Him the name above all names, made Him sit on the right hand of God's throne with glory, and gave Him the authority as the King of kings and the Lord of lords.

Thus, just as Jesus did, you must be able to obey God's will unconditionally in order to have the faith to enter New Jerusalem. The one who can enter New Jerusalem must be able to understand even the depth of God's heart. This kind of person pleases God because he is faithful to the point of death to follow the will of God.

God refines His children to lead them to have faith like gold so that they will be able to enter New Jerusalem. Just as a miner washes and filters in search of gold for a long time, God is keeping His eyes on His children as they change into beautiful souls and wash their sins away with His Word. Whenever He finds children who have faith like gold, He rejoices over all His pains, agony, and sorrow He endured to accomplish the purpose of the human cultivation.

Those who enter New Jerusalem are true children God has gained by waiting a long time until they changed their hearts into the heart of the Lord and accomplished the whole spirit. They are so precious to God and He loves them so much. That is why God urges that, "May your whole spirit, soul and body be kept blameless at the coming of our Lord Jesus Christ" (1 Thess. 5:23).

People fulfilling the duty of martyrdom with joy

Martyrdom is giving up one's life. Thus, it requires a firm determination and great devotion. The glory and comfort one receives after giving up his life to accomplish God's will, the way Jesus did, are beyond imagination.

Of course, everybody who enters the Third Kingdom or New Jerusalem has faith to become a martyr, but the one who actually becomes a martyr receives a much greater glory. If you are not in a condition to become a martyr, you have to have the heart of a martyr, accomplish sanctification, and fulfill your duties completely to receive the reward of a martyr.

God once revealed to me the glory that a minister of my church will receive in New Jerusalem once he fulfills his duty of martyrdom. When he reaches heaven after fulfilling his duty, he will shed endless tears looking at his house in thanks for God's love. At the gate of his house, there is such a big garden with so many kinds of flowers, trees, and other decorations. From the garden to the main building lays the road of gold, and flowers praise the achievements of their owner and comfort him with beautiful scents.

Furthermore, birds with gold feathers shine with lights, and beautiful trees stand in the garden. Numerous angels, all animals, and even the birds praise his achievement of martyrdom and welcome him, and when he walks on the road of flowers his love toward the Lord becomes beautiful aroma. He will continually confess his thanks from his heart saying, "The Lord truly loved me so much and gave me a precious duty! That is why I can stay in the love of the Father!"

Inside the house many precious jewels decorate the walls and the light of carnelian as red as blood and the light of sapphire are extraordinary. The carnelian shows his passionate love and that he accomplished the enthusiasm to give up his life the way the apostle Paul did. The sapphire represents his unchanging, upright heart and his integrity to keep the truth to the point of death. It is for the remembrance of his martyrdom.

On the outer walls is an inscription written by God Himself. It records the times of the owner's trials, when and how he became a martyr, and in what kind of circumstances he accomplished God's will. When people of faith become martyrs they praise God or sometimes speak words to glorify Him. Such remarks are written on this wall. The inscription shines so brightly that you are thoroughly impressed and full of happiness by reading it and looking at the lights coming out from it. How impressive it would be since God, light itself, wrote it! Thus, whoever visits his house will bow in front of those writings written by God Himself!

On the inner walls of the living room are many big screens with many kinds of murals. The drawings explain how he acted since he had first met the Lord, how much he loved the Lord, and the kinds of works he did with what kind of heart at certain times.

Also, in one corner of the garden are many kinds of sports equipments that are made of wondrous materials and that have decorations that are unimaginable on this earth. God has made them to comfort him because he liked sports very much, but gave them up for the ministry. Dumbbells are not made of any metal or steel like on this earth, but are made by God with special decorations. They are like precious stones that shine beautifully. Amazingly, they weigh differently depending on the person exercising with them. These equipments are not used to keep one in shape, but kept like souvenirs as a source of comfort.

How would he feel looking at all these things that God has prepared for him? He had to give up his desires for the

Lord, but now his heart is comforted and he is so thankful for the love of the Father God. He just cannot stop thanking and praising God with tears because God's delicate and caring heart prepared everything he ever wanted, not missing a slightest want in his heart.

People fully united with the Lord and God

In New Jerusalem, God showed me there is a house that is as big as a big city. It was so amazing that I could not help myself from being surprised at its size, beauty, and splendor. This house has twelve gates; three gates on each side—north, south, east, and west. In the center is a big three-story castle decorated with pure gold and all kinds of precious stones.

On the first floor there is such a big hall in which you cannot see the one end from the other, and there are many living rooms. They are used for banquets or as meeting places. On the second floor are rooms to maintain and display crowns, clothes, and souvenirs, and also there are places to receive prophets. The third floor is used exclusively for meeting the Lord and sharing love with Him.

Around the castle are walls that are covered by flowers with beautiful scents. The River of the Water of Life is flowing around the castle peacefully, and over the river are arch-shaped cloud bridges with rainbow colors. In the garden many kinds of flowers, trees, and grass make the perfection of beauty. On the other side of the river is a huge forest beyond imagination.

There is also an amusement park with many rides, such as the crystal train, the Viking-ride made of gold, and other facilities decorated with jewels. They give out delightful lights whenever they are in operation. Beside the amusement park is a wide flower road, and over the flower road is a plain like the tropic plains of this earth, where animals play around and rest peacefully.

Other than these, there are many houses and buildings that

are decorated with many kinds of jewels to shine beautiful and mysterious lights all around the area. Next to the garden, there is also a waterfall, and behind the hill is a sea on which large cruise ships like the *Titanic* sail. All this is a part of one's house, so you can imagine a little how big and wide this house is by now.

This house, which is like a big city, is a tourist spot in heaven, and attracts many people not only from New Jerusalem but also from all over heaven. People enjoy themselves and share the love of God. Also, countless angels serve the owner, take care of the buildings and facilities, escort the cloud automobile, and praise God with dancing and playing musical instruments. Everything is prepared for the utmost happiness and comfort.

God has prepared this house because the owner has overcome all kinds of tests and trials with faith, hope, and love, and has led so many people to the way of salvation with the Word of life and God's power, loving God first and more than anything else.

The God of love remembers all your efforts and tears, and He pays back according to what you have done. And He wants everybody to be united with Him and the Lord with life-giving love and to become spiritual laborers to lead countless people to the way of salvation.

Those who have faith that can please God can be united with Him and the Lord through their life-giving love because they not only resemble the Lord's heart and accomplish the whole spirit, but also give their lives to become martyrs. These people love God and the Lord truly. Even if there were no heaven, they would not regret or feel at a loss for what they could enjoy and take on this earth. They feel so happy and joyful in their hearts to act according to God's Word and to work for the Lord.

Of course, people with true faith live in hope of rewards the Lord will give them in heaven just as it is written in Hebrews

11:6: "And without faith it is impossible to please God, because anyone who comes to him must believe that he exists and that he rewards those who earnestly seek him." However, it does not matter to them whether there is heaven or not, or whether there are rewards or not because there is something more precious. They feel it happier than anything to meet the Father God and the Lord, whom they earnestly love. Therefore, not being able to meet the Father God and the Lord is more misfortunate and sad than not receiving rewards or not living in heaven.

Those who show their undying love for God and the Lord by giving their lives, even if there were no happy heavenly life to look forward to, will be united with the Father and the Lord their bridegroom through their life-giving love. How great the glory and rewards that God has prepared for them will be!

The apostle Paul, who longed for the Lord's appearing and endeavored on the Lord's works and led so many people to salvation, confessed as follows:

> For I am convinced that neither death nor life, neither angels nor demons, neither the present nor the future, nor any powers, neither height nor depth, nor anything else in all creation, will be able to separate us from the love of God that is in Christ Jesus our Lord.
>
> —ROMANS 8:38–39

New Jerusalem is the place for God's children who are united with the Father God through this kind of love. New Jerusalem, clear and beautiful as crystal, where there will be unimaginable, overflowing happiness and joy, is being prepared in such a way.

The Father God of love wants everybody to not only get saved but also resemble His holiness and perfection so that they will come to New Jerusalem.

Therefore I pray in the name of the Lord you will realize that the Lord who went to heaven to prepare rooms for you is coming back soon, and that you will accomplish the whole spirit and keep yourself blameless so that you will become a beautiful bride who is able to confess, "Come soon, Lord Jesus."

ABOUT THE AUTHOR

D R. JAEROCK LEE was born in Muan, Jeonnam Province, Republic of Korea, in 1943. In his twenties, Dr. Lee suffered from a variety of incurable diseases for seven years and awaited death with no hope for recovery. One day in the spring of 1974, however, he was led to a church by his sister, and when he knelt down to pray, the living God immediately healed him of all his diseases.

From the moment Dr. Lee met the living God through that wonderful experience, he has loved God with all his heart and sincerity, and in 1978 he was called to be a servant of God. He prayed fervently so that he could clearly understand the will of God and wholly accomplish it, and he obeyed all the Word of God. In 1982 he founded Manmin Joong-ang Church in Seoul, South Korea, and countless works of God, including miraculous healings and wonders, have taken place at his church.

In 1986 Dr. Lee was ordained as a pastor at the Annual Assembly of Jesus' Sungkyul Church of Korea, and four years later his sermons began to be broadcast on the Far East Broadcasting Company, the Asia Broadcast Station, and the Washington Christian Radio System to Australia, Russia, the Philippines, and many more.

Three years later in 1993, Manmin Joong-ang Church was selected as one of the "World's Top 50 Churches" by *Christian World* magazine. Dr. Lee received an honorary doctorate of divinity from Christian Faith College in Florida, and in 1996 a PhD in ministry from Kingsway Theological Seminary in Iowa.

Since 1993 Dr. Lee has taken the lead in world missions

through many overseas crusades in the U.S., Tanzania, Argentina, Uganda, Japan, Pakistan, Kenya, the Philippines, Honduras, India, Russia, Germany, Peru, and DR Congo. In 2002 he was called a "worldwide pastor" by major Christian newspapers in Korea for his work in various overseas crusades.

As of March 2006, Manmin Joong-ang Church is a congregation of more than 93,000 members and 4,400 domestic and overseas branch churches throughout the globe, and has so far commissioned more than 81 missionaries to 21 countries, including the U.S., Russia, Germany, Canada, Japan, China, France, India, Kenya, and many more.

To this day, Dr. Lee has written thirty-nine books, including bestsellers *Tasting Eternal Life Before Death, The Message of the Cross, The Measure of Faith, Heaven I, Heaven II, Hell,* and *The Power of God.* His works have been translated into more than seventeen languages.

Dr. Lee is currently founder and president of a number of missionary organizations and associations, including chairman of The United Holiness Church of Korea, president of *The Nation Evangelization Paper,* president of Manmin World Mission, founder of Manmin TV, founder and board chairman of Global Christian Network (GCN), founder and president of The World Christian Doctors Network (WCDN), and founder and chairman of Manmin International Seminary (MIS).

OTHER BOOKS BY DR. JAEROCK LEE

Heaven II: Filled With God's Glory
A detailed sketch of the gorgeous living environment the heavenly citizens enjoy in the midst of God's glory

The Message of the Cross
Why is Jesus the only Savior? A powerful, awakening message for all the people who are spiritually asleep. In this book you will find the true love of God.

Tasting Eternal Life Before Death
A testimonial memoir of the Reverend Dr. Jaerock Lee, who was born again and saved from the valley of death.

Hell
An earnest message to all mankind from God, who wishes not even one soul to fall into the depths of hell! You will discover the never-before-revealed account of the cruel reality of the Lower Grave and hell.

The Measure of Faith
What kind of a heavenly place is prepared for you? What kind of crowns will you be rewarded and wear for eternity in heaven? This book provides wisdom and guidance for you to measure your faith and cultivate the best and most mature faith.